D0291709

20 DAYS
TO THE

How the PRECISE Selling Formula
Will Make You Your Company's
Top Sales Performer in 20 Days or Less

Brian Sullivan

SOURCEBOOKS, INC.
NAPERVILLE, ILLINOIS

What People Are Saying
about Brian Sullivan's PRECISE Selling

PRECISE Selling made me rethink everything I knew about sales. I had double-digit sales increases as a result last year, and so far this year I've got triple digit sales increases! Brian—you are a genius!
—Linda Jamison, National Accounts Manager, Time Warner Books

I read like a snail moves and my eyes begin to cross and I usually fall off my chair when reading boring sales books. I am telling you, *20 Days to the Top* is in a completely different category. This is from real world experiences and is something that can be used and measured as I use it day to day.
—Jeff Green, Regular Sales Guy!

I have three words to describe Brian Sullivan's *20 Days to the Top*...Inspiring, Motivating, Entertaining. Those that follow Brian's PRECISE Selling Formula will become famous in their company and industry.
—Gary Fish, CEO, Fishnet Security

We just had the best six months of sales in company history. This trend began twenty days after my sales force committed to Brian Sullivan's PRECISE Selling Formula. Amazing!
—Steven Stolfi, VP of Sales, CCH-CORSEARCH

The PRECISE Selling Formula taught in *20 Days to the Top* has been worth a million. Literally! We just closed on our first $1 million account. This doesn't happen without PRECISE Selling.
—Joe Dager, CEO, Velvet Ice Cream

20 Days to the Top has the exact formula for sales success. And the sales stories in this book are hilarious.
—William Derwin, Director of Marketing, Otis Elevator

Brian Sullivan's PRECISE Selling Formula has been instrumental in creating a company of top performers. This book creates happy customers...and even happier salespeople.
—John Moran, Senior VP of Sales, Welch Allyn, Inc.

Brian Sullivan's PRECISE Selling is best sales training experience I have ever had.
—Earnest Thomas, Eastern Medical & Surgical

Brian demystifies the selling process so salespeople get an understanding of what makes customers say "yes." Several members of my group commented that Brian had given them a new insight into the "black art of selling."
—Don Arnott, General Manager, Everest/VIT Inspection Systems, UK

20 Days to the Top is required reading for all our sales reps...because it works.
—William R. Sparks, President, Med-Tech Associates, Inc.

Without a doubt, you have touched my rep's sales lives. The material and the techniques are right on target, but your masterful delivery and style of impacting a point made it alive to them.
—Yates Farris, VP of Sales, IMCO, Inc.

I have been in hospital sales for over twenty-five years, have participated in numerous sales courses, and read several sales books. Your enthusiasm, passion, and belief in the message you convey are simply unparalleled. You have developed a winning formula!
—Mike Danielson, CEO-Peak Medical

20 Days to the Top is an amazing book and PRECISE Selling really works! I followed everything Brian said and presto, I just got a job with a manufacturer. I used Precise Selling on all of my six interviews to get this job. It is by far the biggest opportunity of my career. One thing is for sure, I will use Precise Selling with every customer, because I want to be my company's top performer...Again!
—Bill Brower, PRECISE Salesperson

Brian reminded me that I don't need to knowledge dump to my customers and they'll tell me all I need to know and more...if I just give them the opportunity and lead the call rather than dominate it!
—Jane Lodwig, Sales, Welch Allyn, UK

Copyright © 2005 by Brian Sullivan
Cover and internal design © 2005 by Sourcebooks, Inc.
Cover photo © Corbis
PRECISE Selling ™ Brian Sullivan
Sourcebooks and the colophon are registered trademarks of Sourcebooks, Inc.

All rights reserved. No part of this book may be reproduced in any form or by any electronic or mechanical means including information storage and retrieval systems—except in the case of brief quotations embodied in critical articles or reviews—without permission in writing from its publisher, Sourcebooks, Inc.

This publication is designed to provide accurate and authoritative information in regard to the subject matter covered. It is sold with the understanding that the publisher is not engaged in rendering legal, accounting, or other professional service. If legal advice or other expert assistance is required, the services of a competent professional person should be sought.—*From a Declaration of Principles Jointly Adopted by a Committee of the American Bar Association and a Committee of Publishers and Associations*

All brand names and product names used in this book are trademarks, registered trademarks, or trade names of their respective holders. Sourcebooks, Inc., is not associated with any product or vendor in this book.

Published by Sourcebooks, Inc.
P.O. Box 4410, Naperville, Illinois 60567-4410
(630) 961-3900
FAX: (630) 961-2168
www.sourcebooks.com

Library of Congress Cataloging-in-Publication Data
      Library of Congress Cataloging-in-Publication Data

Sullivan, Brian.
  20 days to the top : how the precise selling formula will make you your company's top sales performer in 20 days or less / Brian Sullivan.
      p. cm.
  Includes bibliographical references and index.
  ISBN 1-4022-0513-9 (alk. paper)
  1. Selling. I. Title: Twenty days to the top. II. Title.

HF5438.25.S84 2005
658.8'101--dc22

                                                      2005017682

Printed and bound in the United States of America.
VP 10 9 8 7 6 5 4 3

This book is dedicated to my mother, Judy Sullivan,
the most selfless and loving person I have ever known.

Table of Contents

Acknowledgments

20 Days to the Top and the PRECISE Selling Formula is the culmination of fifteen years of real-world sales "lessons" and eight years of trial-and-error sales training. This project would not have been possible without the help of some special people that I will never forget.

I would first like to thank the entire Allyn Family, particularly Penny, Bill, and Dave, for believing in a "not-so-polished" twenty-one-year-old kid with no sales experience and a loud mouth. Your trust and confidence in my ability laid the foundation for the education and sales experiences that became PRECISE Selling and *20 Days to the Top.*

I also want to thank my sales mentors—Gerry Ostrom, Mark Kahling, Jack Disarro, Tony Melaro, John Moran, John Keady, and the many others in the Welch Allyn organization. You taught me countless lessons about what it takes to serve the customer and "wrote the book" on selling, long before this one was conceived. I am still learning from all of you. I would also like to thank Tom McCall and his team for designing the PRECISE Selling logo. You may be in advertising, but your mind is all "sales"!

Thanks also to my sister Tara and brother Bill, who did their best to teach me at an early age the importance of "shutting up." Thanks for the sales lesson...I think! I love you both.

Mom and Dad, I can never thank you enough. Mom, the sacrifices you made for us were the purest form of selflessness and love. Words can't describe how much I miss your guidance. Dad, thanks for showing me, through your example, the importance of taking a risk. Through this book, I just did!

Finally, I want to thank my amazing wife, Leanne, for being my biggest fan. The special moments we share with our two miracles, Jake and Shea, are what drive me to want to be better. While selling is fun, everyday life with you is pure joy...and entertainment! I am the luckiest guy on earth.

I am forever grateful to all of you. Your advice, wisdom, encouragement, and support through the years created this book. It is your gifts to me that I will now share with others in the following pages. Now let's go teach 'em how to be PRECISE!

"Last one to the top is a geriatric."

PART ONE
BUILDING A PRECISE FOUNDATION

This book is divided into two parts. Part One will tell you what it means to be PRECISE. It will also address the essential communication skills you will need to get to the top. Once you finish Part One, Part Two will then "unlock the code" to the seven Actions of the PRECISE Selling Formula. This formula will become your "game day" sales plan and deliver the secrets that separate the top performing "precision-guided sales weapon" from the average rep.

So let's look at Part One as a review of the "blocking and tackling" skills necessary to get to the next level. It is almost impossible to perform well on game day without understanding and practicing these essential communication skills. In this part, you will discover—or perhaps rediscover—the importance of excellent questioning and listening. While these skills *will* help you sell more, they will also make you a more effective communicator in *everything* you do. Whether you are selling your product to a new prospect, your service to a current customer, your leadership vision to an employee, or your parenting thoughts to your children, your success lies in your ability to communicate at a high level. Part One will turn you into a high-level communicator. From there, you will discover new ways to positively influence people's lives.

Oh, and let me be clear. We are going to have a little fun along the way. If you are looking for your typical dry, stale, academic-oriented sales book written by a suit who studied "the art of selling" in an Ivy League classroom, I suggest you close this book immediately. If you're the "work hard/play hard" type who is looking to become famous in your company and industry, let the race to the top begin *right now*.

Chapter One

Your Sprint to the Top Begins with These Easy Steps

Do you want to be your company's top performer? Do you want to be famous in your industry? And do you want to do it quickly? I'm not talking five years, one year, or even six months. How does 20 days sound? Follow these instructions, and it *will* happen. You will improve. You will be PRECISE. You will dominate. And you will be your company's top performer in 20 days...or less.

- Read this book and pay particular attention to sections marked with ⊚
- Internalize the PRECISE Formula of Top Performers.
- Study the seven PRECISE Actions and use them (even if you feel goofy) for 20 days.
- Commit to using the PRECISE Call Sheets (you will learn about these later) every workday for four weeks. (You shouldn't have to think too much about selling on the weekend, should you?)
- Contact me at bsullivan@preciseselling.com if you hit a wall. I will help you smash it.

Do these things, and you will be your company's top performer in 20 days. How do I know? Because I have seen it work for countless salespeople just like you. Keep doing these things, and you will not only be the top performer in your company, but you will be one of the top performers in your industry.

Rookie Reps Can Be PRECISE
Rookies and experienced reps alike can use the techniques you will read in this book. If you are new to sales and you internalize the three Ps that

we will discuss in later chapters, then you will have a leg up on nearly every experienced rep that you will compete against. Why is this? It is because 99 percent of all the salespeople that you will compete against have stagnated. I believe that your sales profession is the easiest to be the best at because so many of the people that you compete against are just plain lame. And I need not worry about offending these folks because they rarely pick up books, attend seminars, or read publications, so they will never see this.

Often you hear, "You need to pay your dues in this business, and that's just going to take some time." I have one response: "Crap." Don't believe this myth for a minute. Your early journey to seasoned sales rep status need not be paved with months of demoralizing speeches like "no pain, no gain." So when "King Experience" fires these demoralizing clichés your way, don't let them bother you. Just do your job, master PRECISE Selling, and outperform the old goat.

Do everything you can to get to the top as quickly as you can. You do not need to be "in the business" for "quite a few years," and you do not need to have walked to your accounts uphill in the driving snow both ways. So at the next sales meeting when "Old Stiffy" tells you it is going to take a long time for you to really "get it," just put a little smile on your face, be humble, and say thanks for the advice. And then go kick his ass where it counts. If he is a peer, show up higher on the list when those sales numbers come out. If she is a competitor, take peace in knowing that she went through hard years that you will never have to. If it is your boss, nod your head, tell her how committed you are, and then quickly become the top dog in her region.

Whatever you do, do not let time be a speed bump to the top. Look at PRECISE Selling as fast-forward button on your early sales career, and look at yourself as new technology. Newer technology is faster and does more than old technology. And it is more PRECISE.

Veteran Reps Can Be PRECISE

"The moving walkway is about to end. The moving walkway is about to end." For anyone who has ever traveled O'Hare airport in Chicago and been lucky enough to be traveling between United Airlines terminals, you no doubt have heard this little chime. A computer voice chats with you as you travel a moving conveyor belt designed to make everybody move faster.

If you have used a moving walkway before, you know what it is like as you approach it. For some, it looks as though they are preparing to jump out of an airplane at high altitude. Well, there is no doubt the body does something a little strange when you get on and off those things. As you first put your feet on the silver belt, you feel a little pull as if you just let go of a rope while playing tug-of-war. But you quickly regroup and just keep walking, happy to find that you are getting to your destination more quickly.

This is how PRECISE Selling will feel to the experienced sales rep that commits to trying the methods taught in this book. She will feel a little tug at first. But as she looks to her right and to her left, she will notice others, not on the walkway, moving their legs a whole lot faster and harder. But because she is on the moving walkway called PRECISE Selling, she is just passing them by.

What is PRECISE Selling?

> "Don't talk so much. You keep putting your foot in your mouth. Be sensible and turn off the flow. When a good man speaks, he is worth listening to. But the words of fools are a dime a dozen."
>
> —Proverbs 10:19–20

PRECISE Selling is a *measurable, repeatable,* and *sustainable* selling behavior that creates happier customers and fatter commission checks. It is saying only what is necessary to inform and excite a customer. While average sales reps speak the words of fools and are a dime a dozen, PRECISE sales representatives say much less but communicate much more. And they know when they have done it well, know how to do it over and over, and know how to keep doing it long after the average sales rep has fallen back to mediocrity.

Take a moment and think about some of your recent experiences as a consumer. Now pick your worst one. Chances are the sales rep was more than socially inept and perhaps did little more than waste your time. This is not to say he or she was a bad father, mother, brother, or sister to somebody. In fact, I am sure there are some people who enjoyed that person's company, but it just was not you. You sit wondering, "How does this person hold a job?" Well, I bet this sales nightmare was anything but PRECISE.

Get to the Point!

Main Entry: pre·cise
Function: adjective
1: exactly or sharply defined or stated
2: minutely exact
3: strictly conforming to a pattern, standard, or convention
4: distinguished from every other

Now I ask you, "When you are being sold to, wouldn't you like this cheese ball in front of you better if those words rolling off his tongue were sharply defined or stated instead of long-winded and dull? Wouldn't it be great if you went to buy that politically incorrect SUV only to find the salesperson on the showroom didn't waste your time but was instead minutely exact. And if by strictly conforming to a pattern or standard, that sales guru was able to make her presentation last fifteen minutes instead of an hour? And what if that same rep was able to distinguish herself from every other rep by selling you only something that you wanted?"

If you said yes to these questions, ask yourself this, "Are the words I am using always exact, sharply defined, and distinguished from the competition?" Come on now, be honest!

> "He can compress the most words into the smallest idea
> of any man I know."
>
> —Abraham Lincoln

You never want a good guy like Honest Abe to speak this way of you, do you? To prevent this from happening, keep asking yourself after every sales call, "Did every word out of my mouth mean something and add value to the customer?"

Saying more in less time is a good thing. If you feel that this might not necessarily be the case in your current sales existence, I assure you PRECISE Selling will sharpen it up. Look at PRECISE Selling as a boot camp for your mind, mouth, and emotions.

What Class of Sales Rep Are You?

Salespeople come in many different flavors, but most of us can be put into one of the following classes.

The Stereotypical Rep is what most people think of when they think of salespeople. These people are pushy, loud, and are the reason the world thinks of us as pains in the backside. The bottom line is that these stereotypical reps talk too much, listen too little, and annoy the hell out of their prospects and current customers. Don't be this class of rep!

Everybody's Friend is another common class of sales rep. This type does everything possible to distance herself from the word "sales." Everybody's Friend does such a good job at not being a salesperson that most of the time that's exactly what her sales numbers show. But she doesn't care, because she has more friends than anybody, is buddies with tons of prospects and customers, tells more jokes than Drew Carey, and cares more about people liking her than about sales results. Everybody's Friend needs to realize that if she wants to be a pleaser, she needs to get out there and sell more stuff. So while you try to do everything possible to make the customer respect and trust you, don't lose sight of your supreme objective.

The PRECISE Sales Rep is not pushy or annoying like the Stereotypical Rep, nor is she wimpy like Everybody's Friend. The PRECISE Sales Rep is:

- Prepared for every sales call
- A builder of respect and trust
- Effective at engaging a customer with questions
- Able to convey the perfect solution that satisfies customers' needs and wants
- Decisive
- Able to stir action in others
- Able to secure agreement and advance a sale
- Always exploring for more business
- Never dull

> "He is not only dull himself, he is the cause of dullness in others."
> —Samuel Johnson

PRECISE Sales Reps Are Enthusiastic

It is nearly impossible to get your customer "fired up" about your product or service if you are not at least showing a moderate amount of enthusiasm about what you are selling. Emotion plays a key role in any call to action, and this is no different as you stand in front of your prospects. Too many sales representatives tell instead of sell. They then cross their fingers in hope that the light bulb will magically turn on above their customer's head. Truth is, if you want to turn on your customer's light bulb, it takes more than a little spark—it takes a whole lot of electricity. This electricity starts with you.

PRECISE Sales Reps are Enthusiastic Leaders

> "Knowledge is power, but enthusiasm pulls the switch! Just remember, the level of excitement in an organization often rises to the level of enthusiasm of the leader."
> —Richard L. Weaver II, Professor, Bowling Green State University

Great leaders make things happen. Think of some of the great leaders in recent history. Martin Luther King Jr., Ronald Reagan, JFK, Vince Lombardi, and countless others had the ability to stir emotion in those that they led. As Ronald Reagan stood at the base of the Berlin Wall, there was nothing dull about the words he used. And when Martin Luther King Jr. uttered the words, "I have a dream," I can assure you he was putting nobody to sleep. While it might be a leap to compare a sales call to these historic moments, it is these moments that can serve as learning experiences about the way people respond to the enthusiasm of those who are speaking. If you want your customer's eyes and ears to be open to your message, you to need to speak as a leader speaks. Speak with enthusiasm.

PRECISE Sales Reps Are Flies

Aristotle was smart. I am not. Having said that, if you give me something that makes sense, I'll try it. And if it works, I will keep doing it until it doesn't work anymore, and then adapt until it does.

I like to compare my brain to that of a fly. As science goes, if you put a bee in a glass jar and lay the jar on its side with the bottom pointed toward a light, then take off the lid, the bee will never escape from the jar. He will keep flying toward the light, believing that it is the only way out. He never adapts and never readjusts. He is programmed to go toward that light and he will die trying. God bless him.

The fly handles things in a much different manner. The bee believes the only way it can reach its goal (the light), is to fly directly toward it. The fly, on the other hand, will smack its head on the back, top, and sides of the jar until it finds a way to get out. Sure, it's a bit painful for the fly, but at least he is willing to try something new. If you are reading this book, chances are you have a little fly in you as well.

Now here is a dose of reality. While learning and using PRECISE Selling, you will get a few bumps on the head. In fact, if you commit to trying the techniques in this book, there will be days that you will wish you *were* a fly. You will walk out of your first three calls saying, "Flies suck, bees are much cooler. I would rather be a bee." Resist this temptation. The sales world has enough worker bees buzzin' around. These are folks that keep flying toward the light, but will never reach their true potential. And in the process, they will bore the hell out of countless customers.

PRECISE Selling is the most repeatable, measurable, and sustainable selling method there is. If you commit to making it mold with that dynamic personality of yours, you will not only achieve your monthly sales objectives, you will blow them out.

PRECISE Sales Reps Don't Live in a Box

Many experienced sales reps box themselves in too early in their careers. They become convinced that they can do their jobs with limited knowledge and minimal effort. Unfortunately, the result is often too much or too little confidence. PRECISE salespeople spend their entire careers making steady, yet often subtle improvements in their "game." To be a top performer, you too must seek out ways to sharpen your skills. You must never let the ceiling of mediocrity prevent you from reaching even higher in your sales career than you ever thought possible.

One story that explains this point best is about flea trainers. Now, I never even knew that flea trainers existed the first time I read this story, but who cares, it's a great story.

Flea trainers have noticed a repeatable, predictable, and unusual habit when they put their specimen in a cardboard box with a lid on it. The fleas will jump as high as possible while hitting their little flea heads on the lid that is keeping the box closed. Now these fleas are not as stupid as you might think. They eventually figure it out and adjust the height of their jump so they no longer hit the lid.

When the flea trainers take that lid off, the fleas will not jump out of the box because they have conditioned themselves to jump only to a certain height. It is this conditioning that keeps them in the box and prevents them from ever getting out.

So often sales representatives act like the flea. The box top can be many things in sales. It can be the fear of rejection. It can be the complacency from too much time in the field. It can be the false sense of success that sometimes comes with success. It can be a demotivating manager. It can be tons of things. Whatever it is, sales professionals like you live in a box and somebody or something is always trying to put the lid on it. The only way to keep that lid open is to keep smashing your head against it. If you do not do this, the lid will close, and you will never jump as high as you possibly can.

PRECISE Sales Reps Don't Give Up

PRECISE sales reps are never negative and avoid negativity at all costs. They are never beaten and have an ability to face rejection and use it to make them better. Consider the achievements of these people who have overcome doubt, rejection, and misfortune.

- Beethoven composed his greatest works after becoming deaf.
- When he was a struggling young artist, Walt Disney was told by a

prospective employer to try another line of work. He said Disney didn't have any creative, original ideas.

- Thomas Edison once spent $2 million developing an invention that never got off the ground.
- In 1962, a recording company executive turned down The Beatles because, "We don't like your sound. Groups of guitars are on their way out."
- Sir Walter Ralcigh wrote *The History of the World* during a thirteen-year imprisonment.
- Christopher Columbus was told that he would sail to his doom and went on to discover new lands.
- Martin Luther translated the Bible while enduring confinement in the Castle of Wartburg.
- Under a sentence of death and during twenty years in exile, Dante wrote the *Divine Comedy.*
- And when President Franklin Roosevelt died in 1945 at the age of 63, he was writing a speech for the upcoming Jefferson/Jackson Day dinner. Suddenly, the president slumped over and fell victim of a cerebral hemorrhage. The last words written on his paper were "The only limit to our realization of tomorrow is our doubts of today."

Well, tomorrow begins right now. It's time to shake any doubts and prepare to become PRECISE. I am about to give you an unfair advantage that will turn you into your company's top performer in 20 days or less.

Chapter Two
Creating PRECISE Selling: How a Proctologist Taught Me a Lesson in Sales

The Journey Begins

To me—twenty-six-years old, a good job, single, and living four houses over the left-field wall of Wrigley Field with an overweight golden retriever named Bailey—life was pure heaven. My life was giving a new meaning to the words "work hard, play hard" and I could not have thought of a better place in the world to live. I often thought of Harry Caray, Chicago icon and longtime famous announcer for the Cubs, as the devil, trying to get me to commit the dreaded sin of attending those 1:20 afternoon ball games.

While I did give in to the temptation on occasion, my supreme objective was to advance within in my sales organization as quickly as possible. I was in my fifth year with Welch Allyn, Inc., a prominent medical device manufacturer, and had experienced a few good years of sales beginner's luck. I led the company in overall percentage increase in my first year, and throughout the following four years was either first or second in every product category. I did all of this despite that fact that I...well...how should I put this...okay, *sucked* as a salesperson. But I wore that suckiness with style and was convinced that I knew just about everything I needed to know about selling. Well, that would all change the day that a proctologist taught me a lesson in sales.

My company had just introduced the latest product, which was a colonoscope. It was the latest and greatest in the world of flexible, video endoscopes used to examine the colon. I became convinced that colon exams were fun. For those of you that have been on the receiving end of a colonoscopy, this might not be the case, but for me as a sigmoidoscope and colonoscope sales representative, it was sheer excitement.

For those first five years of my selling career, I thought that all it took to be a champion sales representative was great product knowledge and a big smile. Now, don't get me wrong, my company had put me through what I thought was a pretty good sales training program, but my response was a typical one. Like most sales reps, I took bits and pieces and only those parts that I thought fit my particular selling style. And like most reps, one year later it was as if I had never been through the program. Like most, I went right back to selling the only way I knew, and that was by acting like a B-52 bomber dropping feature after feature on top of my customer's heads until they submitted.

And therein lies the problem. Almost every sales training program that exists will tell you that the foundation of any sales presentation, or any communication for that matter, is built on the power of questioning. Well, throughout those selling days in Chicago, the only questioning that I did was to ask the receptionist where to set up my video monitor and my friendly scope. After that, my sales "presentation" became a potpourri of statement after statement after statement about all the features that I thought were great about my product.

Graduation Day

Tuesday, November 6, 1996, was the day. I call it graduation day because it was a turning point in my sales existence. It was the beginning of my journey away from being an average salesperson, and one that inspired me to look at the sales profession in an entirely different way.

I had a scope demonstration scheduled at one of the most prominent gastroenterology offices in Chicago. As I walked into the waiting room, I thought I'd taken a wrong turn and wound up at the Ritz-Carlton. This waiting room was plush. After waiting forty-five minutes for my scheduled demonstration, two young, sharp-looking gastroenterologists entered the exam room. Although I was a bit nervous, these two comrades seemed pretty nice and I thought I could handle them. The demonstration was going well from the second I started yapping, and it seemed as if everything I said was resonating with them. The more I spewed my features, the more they loved my product and me. There was absolutely no way in hell I could lose this sale.

Well, after telling them anything and everything I could possibly tell them (regardless of whether or not it interested them), I thought the time had come to go for the close. After stuttering for about fifteen seconds, I said to both of my new friends, "Great, it sounds as if you like the scope. Should I go ahead and ship you one?"

Now, laughter is often a good icebreaker on a sales call; but not when the ice is being broken at your expense. After asking for the order, one of the doctors turned to his friend, turned up his eyebrows, and gave him perhaps the best impersonation of the Joker that I had ever seen. Both doctors then began laughing.

I said to them, "What are you laughing at?"

One of them then turned to me and said, "Brian, we really like your scope, and we think it would probably make sense here in our office. But you see, we have no power…I mean zero power in this office to make any buying decisions."

I said to them, "Well, who does?"

The other doctor turned to me and said, "My father."

I said, "Can we bring your father in here to talk about it?"

Then they both turned to each other and began laughing hysterically. One of the physicians said to the other, "Don't do it to him. I repeat, do not do it to him."

As an eager young sales representative, I was ready to be done and said, "Do it to me, do it to me."

They agreed, and they both walked out the door. Nearly fifty minutes had gone by before I had seen anyone venture past the exam room door. And then there he was…all five-feet-one of him. And though he was short, there was no doubt in my mind that I was standing in front of one of the toughest old SOBs that I had ever faced. He was bald, scaly, had biceps like Popeye the Sailor Man, and to him I looked like a large can of spinach.

Despite having just soiled my underwear, I thought that I had better start talking or I would be in even deeper. And so I did. Like with his son and partner before him, I continued the barrage of bells and whistles hoping that he too would succumb to my sales pressure. As he stood there with his arms, lips, eyebrows, and nasal hairs folded, I thought for sure he had to like what I was saying. Regardless, it didn't bother me one way or another, because I was on a mission. And the words were just flowing out of my mouth as if I had just stolen an enema from the exam room drawer and put it in my mouth.

At no time did my new prospect change facial expressions or posture…until he could take no more. Throughout the previous fifteen minutes of verbal diarrhea, I made statement after statement after statement about what I thought he needed in his practice. At no time did I think to question him about what he thought he needed. Had I shut up for just ten seconds and looked at his expression, I would have known that things were not going very well. It was only when I made my final statement that he had had enough.

I began discussing the ability of my product to take pictures of the colon for medical record keeping. This was a feature on my product that I was very excited about, and when I spoke about it, I spoke with great conviction. I said to him, "Every GI practice like yours needs a video printer to store images should there ever be concerns about litigation or malpractice." Oops. Not good!

Popeye had heard enough. He slowly walked over to me and stopped roughly two inches from my nose. He took a deep breath and said, "Son, I've looked up more assholes in my day than you have hairs on your head."

I didn't know what to do. I felt like a bear was staring me down and if I made one false move, I would be dead. So I did what came naturally, I began laughing. But this was a painful laugh, because I was doing everything possible to keep my lips together so he would not think that I was being disrespectful. It looked like I had a terminal case of the hiccups.

He then said, "Why are you laughing?"

And I responded, "Because that was funny?"

As he said to me, "Funny how?" (I could have sworn that I had been beamed into the movie Goodfellas, and that Joe Pesci was going to take a gun out and shoot my foot off any minute.)

I said to him, "That was the funniest thing I ever heard from a customer." And then he started chuckling.

Well, it ended up that Popeye was just a sarcastic old-timer that loved to give salespeople a hard time. To him it was a test—and one I failed miserably. He later went on to tell me that I should have asked him some questions about what he thought before boring him with what I thought. It was the greatest sales lesson I had heard up to that moment, but it was a lesson that I had heard in the sales classroom already several times.

Perhaps the only reason it finally sunk in was because it was coming from the only person that really matters, and that's the customer.

Split Me in Thirds

There is an old rule in sales. That rule states that one-third of the people that you present your solution to will buy from you regardless of how bad you are as a sales rep. Another third will never purchase from you regardless of how dynamic your personality is or how perfect your solution may be. It is that one-third in the middle that you are fighting for. Well, that day in Chicago, I actually walked out of the building with an order in my hand, although I asked no questions, made dozens of statements, and showed no ability to listen to the customer's needs. My reward for ineptness was a signature and a down payment telling me the miserable job that I had just done was good enough.

This contradiction in feelings happens to sales reps all the time. We often perform poorly and are still rewarded with sales numbers and commission checks that falsely tell us that we are doing just fine. What we don't realize is that it is only the easy one-third that we are most often getting when we are not effectively questioning, listening, and conveying our solution to the people we serve. With PRECISE Selling, you will achieve the skills necessary to not only capture the low-hanging fruit, but to dominate your competition in that middle one-third battleground.

Never Plateau in Your Profession

I learned a scary but valuable sales lesson from that proctologist. After walking out of that office, I was not sure if I should be elated to have an order in my hand or discouraged because I had just been "found out." For five years straight I had consistently been my company's top performer in capital equipment sales, and rarely during those five years did I take time to consider that I was not performing to the best of my sales ability.

The upside of my pathetic, statement-driven, feature-and-benefit-spewing sales style was that there was only one way to go and that was up. After that sales call, I wouldn't let my past success convince me that I was anything more than average. I realized that day that I had plateaued in my profession, and that plateau was nowhere near the top of the mountain. Things were about to change. I was about to make a commitment to learn everything I could about selling. What makes successful salespeople tick?

What are their habits? How do they think? How do they feel? How do they face rejection? I couldn't get enough. It was time to go to the next level.

That sales call on Popeye and the research that followed paid off. It was the following year that I was awarded the President's Cup, recognizing the company's top attitude, aptitude, and performance. What made me most proud about this award is that it was not just about sales numbers. In fact, sales numbers were not even the most heavily weighted factor in winning it. Attitude was the most important pillar for a Welch Allyn salesperson, and the fact that the sales leaders thought that I did my job with character was an honor. Winning the President's Cup opened doors within my company, and I couldn't wait for more responsibility. And I owed it all to Popeye the Procto Man.

Time to Step It Up

Then the big day came. The national sales manager at the time asked me and two other colleagues with a history of high sales performance to begin doing research on the many sales training programs that existed on the market. He too had realized that we needed to serve our customers better by "learning" how to serve our customers better. It would be our job to become the sales reps that would train our peers. His goals seemed simple. Take what he called the C players and make them B's, and take the B's and make them A's. As I asked what to do with the A's he told me, "Just don't screw 'em up."

My two counterparts and I researched and examined almost every selling skills program that existed on the market. We were looking for something that would allow us to still be ourselves, but also help us improve from top to bottom when in front of the customer. We weren't looking for a flaky sales program to help increase our self-esteem, or one that shows how the state of our karma directly impacts our capacity to overcome objections. In short, we were sales-course skeptics looking for reasons to mock everything that we read and saw. We found much to mock, but to our surprise we settled on some material that was very much "how to."

There were several systems with similar fundamentals that we could buy into, so we did. Soon after, my two cronies and I made our way to a three-day sales seminar and the journey began. While we did not take all the material our toupee-wearing instructor was throwing at us, we took much of it. It would become the foundation that we would build our program on. We believed if we internalized these teachings, we would do a better job serving our customer and in the end, a better job serving our company and ourselves.

It Worked!

Seminar day was finally here, but my two buddies and I were no longer students, we were now teachers. We had taken all that we had learned, combined it with real-life experience, customized it to our daily lives and what we were selling, and off we went. At the time, our sales on our most important product, the colonoscope, were not great. We were hoping the sales training we were about to attempt would provide the needed kickstart to get the numbers up. So eight guinea pigs from various parts of the country flew to Chicago for the main event and attended our first class. We printed booklets and award certificates and polished the shiny new selling school trophy. We were good to go!

While our presentation skills were not of Zig Zigler quality, they were good enough to fire up the reps. It was only when one of my students came up to me over dinner one night that I had heard my first area of concern. This would not normally faze me, but this rep was a guy named Dave—as in Dave Allyn, whose family owned the company. He said, "I don't think this will work in my territory. People down south are more laid-back. They don't like to be sold." After testing some of my new skills on how to overcome objections, Dave agreed that he would at least try it. Whew!

Twelve months and a few seminars later, we found ourselves sitting pretty. We no longer had the famously clichéd 80/20 rule (20 percent of reps sell 80 percent of the product) working, and there was little doubt the tide had turned. Before our year of sales training, we had a small group of sales studs selling most of our product. One year after training, most of our sales force was now enjoying the party. In fact, we went from 20 percent of the reps selling 80 percent of our product to 65 percent selling 80 percent of our product.

When the product manager for the scope products approached me and told me of these numbers, I could only say, "Um, can you translate that? What's this 80, 20, 80, and 65? Do I need to remind you that I am a sales guy?" He said, "Sully, the selling skills are working. Many of our C players are now B players. There are a bunch of B folks turning A on us. And everybody is pumped that you guys didn't screw up the top-performing A team."

That day confirmed just how fun the sales profession could be. It also gave me an early glimpse of the immense enjoyment that comes with helping turn salespeople into top performers.

Evolution

Over the next seven years, Welch Allyn grew at a good clip as acquisitions and research and development dollars rose. As we entered new markets with more complex customers and more multitiered selling situations, our selling skills also had to evolve. As I took the role of full-time sales trainer, I would now have more time to study diverse markets and customer and rep behavior. From there I would adapt what we taught to what would best serve our customer and, of course, our top line sales numbers.

This evolution would give us PRECISE Selling. I believe PRECISE Selling combines the best tried-and-true sales principles with some real-life "meat" the average sales rep can get his arms around. I will not kill you with theory, fluff, or selling skills from the academia. I am a salesperson—always have been and always will be. I will teach you what I have seen change my sales life and the sales lives of dozens of people from many diverse industries. This stuff works! After reading this book, you will have the specific tools to be your company's top performer...in 20 days or less.

Chapter Three
Fishing for Contrarians:
How to Sell in a World of Mopes

There is a very good sales book written by Thomas Freese called *Question-Based Selling.* In it, he references a story that Dale Carnegie used to tell back in the 1930s. In this story, Dale tells us how every summer he liked to go fishing up in Maine. And while he was fishing, he would sit on the dock and eat strawberries and cream. But he found that fish did not like strawberries and cream, fish preferred worms. So while he was hanging out on that dock, he did not think about what he liked, but instead, thought about what fish liked. He did not bait his hook with strawberries and cream, instead he dangled a worm or a grasshopper in front of them, and said, "Wouldn't you like to have that?"

Selling Is Fishing

What is the message that Dale Carnegie is trying to tell us? It seems simple. When you are selling, it is essential that you bait your sales hook not with things that you like, but instead with what the customer likes. And just because you love specific features about your product, service, or sales promotion, don't think the customer should feel the same way. I know it's hard to believe, but most customers are not dying to hear what you think. But as obvious as this may seem, most salespeople overlook this fact while standing in front of their prospects.

Information Overload

As a sales rep, you are bombarded with new product information, new statistics, new marketing material, and countless other information that is supposed to help you better serve your customer. It is your job to weed through all the information, and keep in the forefront of your mind only those benefits that are going to be important to your customer. Once you do this, it is then your job to develop your own opinions about the information that you hear.

Let's say you learn about a new product during a sales meeting. You pick up a sheet of literature, look at it, read about all the features and benefits, and wrap a little logic and thought around what you are seeing. You then read a little more and perhaps think of four or five current customers that you think would love this product. You then pick up your product (assuming it is tangible), and begin adding a little emotion and excitement to the mix. In essence, what you are doing is building your own strawberry. That strawberry has become the bait that you will use to reel in your customer.

This is not necessarily a bad thing. As a sales rep, you are expected to develop an opinion about the things you will sell. But it is how you use that logic and emotion that makes the difference between being PRECISE and being average. The average sales rep takes that strawberry, puts it on the fishing hook, and casts it out with a fishing pole made up of many statements. Statements, especially within the first few minutes of a sales call, carry with them tons of risk.

Statements Can Push People Away
The PRECISE sales rep speaks less and makes fewer statements than the average sales rep. In my position as a sales trainer, I am able to sit back and watch hundreds of sales calls each year. In my travels, I see a direct correlation between the amount of statements and the amount of success in each call. The more statements that a sales rep makes, the less success he or she will have. Why is this?

The Contrarian
When you make statements in a conversation, the natural tendency of the person being spoken to is to be a "Contrarian."

Main Entry: con·trar·i·an
Function: noun
1a: somebody disposed to taking opposite position; somebody who is prone to opposing policies, opinions, or accepted wisdom

In the PRECISE Selling world, the Contrarian does not always oppose everything that is said to him. Sometimes instead of blurting out the completely opposite viewpoint he will throw you a bone, agree with you, but then add on to what you said just to make sure his opinion was thrown into the mix. It's just a nice little game of one-upmanship. Here are some examples of how a conversation with a Contrarian might sound.

Your statement: Spring is right around the corner.

The Contrarian: Yeah, but that stupid groundhog says we have six more weeks of winter misery.

Your statement: PRECISE Selling has really helped me stay focused in sales calls.

The Contrarian: Yeah, but I have been selling for sixteen years now, and I don't buy into any of that sales guru crap.

Why Are We Contrarians?

Whose opinion do we love the most? *Our own*...and customers are no different. Customers would most certainly prefer to have their opinions dominate a sales call instead of the sales rep's. When you make a statement about your product or service, where is that statement coming from? Well, obviously your mouth, but it started at your brain. Your statement is an expression of *your* opinion. And whose opinion is most important in a sales call? Correct...the customer's! When you are trying to get somebody happily involved in your product or service, let their thoughts and opinions—not yours—dominate the sales conversation. Limiting the number of statements you make will allow this to happen.

Suburban Contrarian

I began studying the Contrarian Theory in 1999. While I did believe that people have a tendency to be Contrarians, I questioned just how often it occurred. And even if it did occur, what effect did it have on my sales calls and the sales reps that I coached?

March brings new life to Shawnee, Kansas. The Autumn Park subdivision is like so many other cul-de-sac-laden neighborhoods strewn across the Midwest, but in that March of 2001, it became my psychology lab. One day, as the temperature rose and the flowers began to bud, scores of neighbors began the yearly battle to see whose lawn and landscaping would look the best that year.

On that day, the neighbors on each side of my house were both outside working on their lawns. Scott, otherwise known as "Mr. Positive," lived on the left side of my house and had fired up his fancy green Lawn Boy lawn mower with that same familiar smile that he loved to show off. It didn't matter if it was raining, snowing, or wind blowing; Scott was going to put a positive spin on anything and everything he could. You know these people. They are so positive all the time that they make you sick.

Specimen #1

As he turned off his lawn mower, I approached Scott for a little small talk. Little did he know that he was my specimen. The goal of my science project was to make a statement to Mr. Positive and see if he acted like a Contrarian. So I fired away.

Me: "I'll tell you what, Scott. It's nice to finally be out of the house doing yard work after being locked up for four cold months."

Mr. Positive: "You know, Brian, I am not sure I am ready for eight months of hard landscaping labor."

Wow, he did it! He made a negative comment in reaction to my positive comment. Even Mr. Positive had the ability to be a Contrarian. I was one for one in my study.

Specimen #2

Specimen number two would not be so easy. While Scott, who lived on my left, was busy spreading love and happiness around the neighborhood, Susan and Connie, who lived on the opposite side of my house, were exactly that...opposite. The angry women that shared a home were two female versions of Ebenezer Scrooge. Nonetheless, it was my scientific duty to fire off a statement to one of them and to study the reaction.

As I motored my Lawn Boy to the other side of my backyard, I slowly looked up to notice Susan (the really mean one) slouched over in her usual Shrek-like pose while working on her rock garden. I turned off my lawn mower, wiped the sweat from my brow, and went in.

I threw a nervous smile on my face and posed a casual greeting to

Susan. Her first response was one of pure shock, and her second was that old familiar scowl that I had grown to love and sometimes cultivate. I froze up and could not think of a good statement to use on Susan, so I just stole the one Scott had just used on me.

Me: "Hey, Susan!"

Susan: (scowl)

Me: "I am not sure if I am ready for eight months of hard landscaping labor."

Susan: (scowl turns to frown, then turns to big fat smile) "You know, Brian, I like to think of yard work as therapy."

Now, I knew Susan needed therapy, but what did she just say? Talk about a Contrarian half-nelson! When I made a whining, negative statement to her, she had two choices to make. She could either agree with me (which would go against everything she stood for), or she could play the role of Contrarian (even if it meant she had to make a positive statement delivered with what was no doubt the most painful smile she ever had to conjure up).

Scientific Conclusion

I made two statements, and both were met with Contrarian responses. As a result, there was little connection between my specimens and me. We each had our own opinions (as trivial as the topic might have been) and those opinions were king in the backyards of Autumn Park. Because I was spreading my opinion around instead of asking their opinion first, there was a disconnection. They may very well have felt exactly as I did, but because I led with my opinion, they chose to be Contrarians. This caused a disconnection between us.

Think about a sales call. Aren't you looking for a connection between your customer and you? If so, statements are not the best way to create it. Get in their heads first, before you start sharing what's in yours.

Negative People Are More Contrarian

As we saw in our scientific suburban experiment, both positive and negative people have the ability to mismatch a statement. However, who do you think has a tendency to be more Contrarian? Of course, negative people thoroughly love their Contrarian qualities. Now let me ask you a question.

Are there any negative customers in your industry? Regardless of whom I am teaching, everybody believes the customers in their industry are more negative than any other.

I know the medical industry that I still serve, made up of doctors, nurses, medical technicians, and receptionists, has an inclination to shy a little toward the negative side. Correct that—it's just plain loaded with people ready and willing to bite a salesperson's head off unless the rep bribes them with some butt-kissing handout.

Customers don't hide their negativity. In fact, we can find visible clues of this Contrarian-like behavior all over the workplace. And yet, we sales-people walk in the door every day oblivious to them. These clues are telling us that they are negative, which means they are Contrarians, which means we better *watch out* and be careful with the number of statements we make.

Two years ago I spent eight months in search of such negativity in the workplace and found it in the form of photocopied and electronic slogans and cartoons. You know, the ones that are tacked up on 4x4 cubicles, hanging on refrigerators, proudly displayed as screen savers telling us just how crappy people's days are going. Let me share with you some of the clues of negativity that I found.

The Neg-ceptionist
This first one comes to us from a receptionist and gatekeeper in Lenexa, Kansas. She displayed it prominently on her computer screen for everyone to see. She tells us:

I go from 0 to bitch in 4.3 seconds.

Do you think she's negative? How do you think she would react to statements of your opinion? I know she didn't give a damn about mine. But if you really feel the urge to spew a bunch of statements to the Neg-ceptionist, you better get your point out in about 3.9 seconds…long before she goes bitch on you.

The Office Mangler—I Mean Manager

Blame, blame, blame. You know these people. The folks that just love to pass the buck. This one comes to us from just such a person in Scottsdale, Arizona. This office manager treated me badly, but it was nothing in comparison to how she treated her colleagues. As I tried skillfully to present my solution to her, I noticed a big, bright, orange flyer telling me:

> Poor planning on your part does not create an emergency on my part.

Hmm, do you think she's a little negative? At that point I had no doubt that she too had the ability to go from 0 to bitch in 4.3 seconds. In fact, she did it more quickly than that and with even a little more moxie than the receptionist.

Oh, and by the way, don't make any statements to this type of office manager. She will not only disagree with you, she will blame you for something you didn't do.

The Wounded

Seattle is a lovely place known for its occasional rainy and sometimes depressing weather. Well, this biomedical engineer was definitely feeling the negative energy that sometimes comes with forty-five straight days of rain. As I tried to strike up a conversation with this non-decision-maker, I noticed an inspirational message taped to his refrigerator.

> Life sucks and then you die.

And directly below it was an even more inspirational message that said:

> Life is a series of disappointments followed by death.

Holy cow! Unless you are selling an all-expense paid trip to visit with Dr. Phil for a little quiet time, you don't have a chance making statements to a guy like this. He's negative. He's a Contrarian. And he's waiting for you to tell him the glass is half-full so he can come back and tell you the glass is half-empty.

The Unifier

In every industry there are certain employees that are obsessed with process. Absolutely everything has to be done according to the written plan, authorized by the joint commission, and certified by some third-party that identifies itself with an acronym. (OSHA, CLIA, ASHA, SUPERCALIFRAGALISTICEXPIALIDOCIOUS, whatever). Well, it was in Omaha, Nebraska, where I met such a person. This fine woman was the "kingpin" of a large medical system, and she was very detail-oriented. She had an instruction manual that she dealt out to her employees for almost everything they did. This is one that she faxed off to all of her kingpin counterparts throughout Nebraska. She wanted to make sure that they had standardized the way they treated salespeople. These were her instructions:

HOW TO GREET A SALESPERSON

1) Extend either arm at an approximately 90° angle perpendicular to the body.

2) Bend arm at the elbow. Position it parallel to the body, forming three sides of a perfect square.

3) Close palm tightly.

CENSORED 4) Fiercely upturn digit between pointer and ring finger.

CENSORED

5) Hold approximately 10 seconds to a minute for emphasis.

What do you think? This seems funny, but this Contrarian was dead serious about how she wanted her staff to treat folks like you and me. Fact is, we will never win a Contrarian like this over with endless statements driven by our own opinions.

Your World

If your industry has people like this, then keep this in mind.

- Negative people are Contrarians.
- Contrarians react oppositely to statements.
- Statements can foster a customer disconnect.
- Customer disconnection is not a good thing.

So be careful about how much of your opinion you share, especially early on in a call. Because of a customer's inherent skepticism of salespeople, the more statements you make, the more chance you give him to share an opposite opinion. So the next time you are just dying to tell your Contrarian customer how your solution is the largest and most powerful on the market, be prepared to have him respond with, "Oh, I don't like big widgets. They have a tendency to break more easily." Whether they truly believe what they say doesn't matter, all that will matter at this point is that the two of you may be heading in opposite directions.

But I Have to Make Some Statements, Don't I?

Okay, okay, I do understand that you must eventually make some statements. You can't just stand there holding your product in your hand, pointing at it, doing everything you can to keep your mouth shut for fear of making a statement that your customer will resist. You will have to make some statements, but only after you ask questions, listen with energy, and receive enough information to help you customize your presentation.

The next chapter will discuss the value of questions. While sales statements often cause prospect disconnect, sales questions are the key to communication and are essential for PRECISE communication.

Chapter Four
Questions, Questions, and Questions: Three Hearing Aids for Your Prospects

"Everybody has three ears: one on the left side of his head, one on the right, and one in his heart."

—Armenian proverb

To be PRECISE, you need to appeal to your prospect's logic and emotion. It is much like selling to two major decision-makers even if you are only presenting to one person. If both decision-makers stuck in that one body are not in unison, chances are you won't be walking away with an order or a follow-up appointment. The key to the ears of the head and of the heart begins with questions.

Why Ask Questions?

As you know, magnets have two sides to them. If you take two magnets and put them together, they will either come together or resist each other. As the old phrase goes, opposites attract and the only way to get two magnets together is to make sure those magnets are lined up correctly.

In a sales call, you and your customer are two magnets and only one of two things is going to happen when you meet. You are either going to come together or you are not. Before you speak, think about which side of the magnet you want to use. Your magnet has two sides. One side is made up of statements and the other is made up of questions. If you want to consistently and magnetically attract your customers, then you must use the "question" side of the magnet more than the "statement" side.

Questions Get Them to Tell You What They Want and Need

Average salespeople tell customers what they should want and need. The PRECISE salesperson asks customers what they want and need, and then delivers PRECISE presentations focused only on fulfilling those wants and needs.

Questions Reduce Resistance

Word: resistance
Function: noun
1a: the act of standing firm against a person or influence

How do you feel when you are being sold? Do you stand firm and keep your walls up? Do you have a tendency to be skeptical of what the sales reps say to you? I know I do, and I teach sales reps every week. Hell, I *am* a salesperson and I have a tendency to despise the very people that do what I do every day. The truth is that most of us are resistant to the statements that salespeople make. Statements cause resistance, but questions allow the customer to feel more in control of the selling situation.

Questions Reduce Risk

Consider the following two approaches:

Risky statement: "The best feature about the unit is that it is small and portable."

Contrarian response: "I don't like small and portable units. They have a tendency to get stolen."

Risk-free question: "Do you like units that are small and portable, or would you prefer a stationary system?"

Risk-free response: "I usually prefer stationary systems that won't get stolen, but if there is enough value packed into a portable unit, I might be willing to give one a look."

Can you see how wording something in the form of a question removes any risk of saying something the customer does not agree with? Before you make a statement on anything, ask a question.

Questions Make Customers Feel in Control

Customers feel in control when they are talking. When you ask questions of your customers, you are inviting them to talk. The more they talk, the more in control they feel. The more in control they feel, the more comfortable they are, and the more willing they will be to bring down the defenses that make it difficult for you to do your job.

Questions Give the Salesperson Control

Lawyers are notorious for manipulating their witnesses with questioning techniques. Turn on Court TV, watch for twenty minutes, and you will see just how good some attorneys are at subtly "leading" a witness. The key word here is subtle. The most successful attorneys are ones that empathetically question their witness, get them to share information, and then help lead them to the attorney's predetermined conclusion.

While it pains me to have to compare our noble vocation to the law profession, there are some likenesses. The most successful salespeople, like the most successful lawyers, use questions to help control and lead their customers to a conclusion. Of course, that conclusion usually means the salesperson has an order in his hand. An example of this type of question follows.

Let's say you just did a presentation on how your product is the smallest and lightest on the market. You hand it to the customer and his eyebrows and lips give an approving look of agreement. Try a leading question such as, "There is quite a size and weight difference from the product you are used to using, isn't there?"

The agreement that follows is fueling the progress of the presentation.

Questions Get Them Fired Up

When great leaders, speakers, and motivators want to get their audience fired up, they do it by asking a question that demands a response. Evangelical ministers are masters at using questions to stir emotions in their congregations. If you ever have attended one of these services or have seen one on TV, you know that when the pastor asks, "Can I get an amen?" The response is usually a resounding, "Amen!" And if that pastor wants to stir just a little more emotion, he will ask again. "I said…could I get an *amen!*" And if he has to ask twice, watch out, that second amen will blow the doors off heaven.

When looking to stir similar emotions from your clients, use those leading questions with emotion. Sound excited when you ask, "There is quite a size and weight difference from the product you are used to using, isn't there?" While the content of the question is important, the way you ask it is just as critical. Do it well, and you too will "blow the doors off" of your presentation.

Questions Allow Customers to Sell Themselves

Salesperson: "How do *you* think the product will make your life easier?"

Customer: "Well, I really think it is going to save me tons of time and . . ."

Prospects can sell themselves even better than salespeople can. So use questions to get prospects to do your job for you. Ask them a question that forces them to tell you why they think your solution is so great.

Questions Prepare Them to Sell to Others

In today's complex selling environment, there are often many tiers of decision-makers. Gatekeepers are often successful in putting up road-blocks that prevent you from getting to the person or people that can pull the trigger. Sometimes the best you can do is to turn your lower-level decision-makers into fine-tuned selling machines by asking them questions that will better prepare them to deliver your message.

Salesperson: "Mary, what part of our solution do you think will resonate most with the CEO?"

Customer: "Well, I think he will love the added efficiency the system will bring, as well as . . ."

When customers start thinking, they start talking. When they start talking, they are practicing to sell your solution up the chain of command.

Questioning Yourself Will Give You Confidence

Confidence is essential in sales, and the first person that needs to be sold on any product or service is *you*. So before you ever enter your first call on any new product or service, ask yourself the questions that your potential customers might ask you. Play devil's advocate in as many ways as possible. If you don't have the answers to your own questions, find them. Once you are able to answer most of your own questions, you will then feel more certain in your early sales calls. When an area of concern comes up, you will not look like a deer in headlights.

Types of Questions

Now that you know the importance of questions, let's look at the different types of questions you can use.

Fact-Finding Questions

Fact-Finding Questions are questions that invite a yes or no response from your customer. They are specific, closed-ended, and do not require much thought. Below are some examples of effective Fact-Finding Questions.

Seller: "Do you have money in this year's budget set aside for software upgrades?"

Prospect: "No, we do not."

Seller: "You did mention there is a real need. Is there any way to find the proper funding?"

Prospect: "Yes, there is."

Fact-Finding Questions are effective in helping you be PRECISE in a sales call. If the prospect in the above example answers no to the question about the customer's ability to find the funding, would it make sense to launch into your product presentation? No, because you could have the greatest product in the world, but there would be no money to pay for it. If you want to get to the bottom of something, just ask a close-ended Fact-Finding Question.

While Fact-Finding Questions can be effective in helping you get some valuable information during a sales call, they are only one questioning tactic necessary to help you design your precision presentation. Be careful not to use too many of this type of question. You do not want your customers to feel as if they are being interrogated.

Barbara Walters Questions (BW Questions)

- Who
- What
- Why
- When
- Where
- How

These are your classic opened-ended questions and are the most valuable questioning tool because they encourage your customer to open up and share valuable information. I call them Barbara Walters Questions because this master interviewer has as an uncanny ability to get an interviewee to respect and trust her. Once she does this, she then uses these types of questions to get her "subject" to open up and share information and emotions.

She is usually successful in breaking down the walls, even though most interviewees (like the customers you serve every day) go into the interview (sale) hoping to keep their thoughts and emotions close to the vest. They often promise themselves that they will share as little information as possible. The top interviewers like Barbara Walters use many open-ended questions to delve deeper into the thoughts and emotions of the people they interview.

Some examples of BW Questions are listed below:

- "Who as well as yourself will be involved in the decision-making process?"
- "What got you interested in taking a look at our product?"
- "When do you think it would make sense to follow up with you?"
- "Why do you think your staff members are having trouble with your current product?"
- "Where did you learn about our services?"
- "How often would you use a product like ours?"
- "What do you think are the greatest benefits of our product?"

Questions like these will get you much information. Use them often, and watch your customers open up and share more of themselves than ever before.

When using BW Questions, do what all great interviewers do. They will never ask just one opened-ended question about a specific topic. They will delve further into that topic by following up with a second and third open-ended question. This is how they are able to get to the real thoughts and emotions of the person they are interviewing.

BW-Effect Questions

It is not enough to know that a customer is not happy with their current supplier. By asking a BW Question, you can find out what it is that they don't like. The average rep stops there and just launches into a presentation about how his product or service can make the prospect happier. But the PRECISE sales rep follows up with another question to find out exactly what effect those things are having on the customer. I call these BW-Effect Questions. Here is an example of the two questions at work:

Salesperson: "Mary, what don't you like about your widget?" (BW Question)

Customer: "It is way too slow."

Salesperson: "What effect is the slow speed having on your ability to conduct your job?" (BW-Effect Question)

Some other examples of BW-Effect Questions are as follows:

• Who does this affect?
• What effect does this have on…?
• When will this affect…?
• Why will this affect…?
• Where will this affect…?
• How does this affect…?

BW and BW-Effect Questions are essential questioning methods that will get your prospects to open up and tell you the information that you will need to better serve them.

Little Yes Questions
…couldn't it? *or*…couldn't you?
…shouldn't it? *or*…shouldn't you?
…wouldn't it? *or*…wouldn't you?
…isn't it? *or* …aren't you?

A Little Yes Question is a statement that ends with a confirmation question that is designed to get the customer to say yes. These types of questions have been used effectively for generations and have been discussed in several sales books and seminars through the years. I love using them at least a couple of times (but no more than that) during the same call. What makes them so effective is their ability to create emotion and involvement in the customer about your product or service.

Some examples of Little Yes Questions are listed below:

- "It could help save you lots of time, couldn't it?"
- "You should be happy long after making a decision as important as this, shouldn't you?
- "The product seems easy to use, doesn't it?"
- "You would like to make sure you're getting the best quality, wouldn't you?"
- "This product is easy to use, isn't it?

When using these kinds of questions, make sure that your first statement is one that will invite a yes response. Once you start getting a few Little Yeses, you will find it much easier to get that *big fat yes* at the end of your seven PRECISE Actions.

Another great thing about these types of questions is they force you to constantly check your progress with your customers. While average sales reps are just spewing features and benefits and stealing the show, it will be your questioning techniques that will help build the emotion of your customer and keep them involved in what you are saying.

Two-Choice Questions

A Two-Choice Question is a question that gives your prospect two acceptable choices to choose from. I have found this question especially effective when using a trial close and while Securing and Advancing (PRECISE Action # 6), which we will discuss later in the book.

Some examples of Two-Choice Questions:

- "Would you like to set up our follow-up appointment for (Choice #1) later this week or would (Choice #2) next week work better for you?"
- "Will the funding be available on this year's budget cycle or next year's?"
- "Would you like to install the product in this room or is there another room that you were thinking of?"

What I like about these questions is they:
- Make "asking for the order" easy
- Allow the customer to still feel in control
- Are effective in advancing a sale

Detail Questions

After a customer says yes to your solution, there are usually some details that need to be worked out. These can be questions about accessories, finances, training, and final location or installation of product, for example. A Detail Question is a question that asks for specifics that would only be needed if the customer were to buy what you were selling. Here is an example:

Let's assume you are selling personal computers and your customer has given you several buying signals. A Detail Question is a great trial close in this situation.

Salesperson: "I am glad you like the product and are happy with the price. Will you be installing it yourself or would like us to help you with that?"

To "test the waters," use Detail Questions that show an assumption that your customers are going to buy your solution. Notice how this Detail Question takes new prospects from sales call to post-sale detail. If they answer your question in an informative way, proceed under the assumption that they are moving forward. If they slow you down, that's okay. At least you now know what they are thinking.

Clarifying Question

A Clarifying Question is one you ask in response to a customer's question. It helps refine exactly what the customer means. For instance:

Customer: "I am a bit concerned because I have never heard of your company."

Sales Rep: "I can understand your hesitation, but can you help clarify what specific areas might concern you, so I can better address them?"

A Clarifying Question can also be a helpful response to a question that needs refining. For instance:

Customer: "Will the computer systems come standard with printers?"

Sales Rep: "Are you going to need printers for all of your computers?"

Whenever your customers ask you a question, pause for a moment and, unless you are 100 percent confident that you know exactly what they are asking, ask a Clarifying Question.

Don't Let Them Fool You

The questioning methods listed above have been used by generations of effective salespeople and taught by generations of sales trainers. There is a new generation of authors and sales trainers that would tell you that these questioning techniques are tired and outdated. Don't buy it. Remember, the objective of PRECISE Selling is to teach you how to better serve your customers by saying less and delivering more. The questioning methods listed above are effective in helping you do this. These questions will get you the wanted information that you need to deliver a sharp, exact, PRECISE presentation.

How Can You Remember These Questions?

I know what you are thinking by now. How can you remember all the questioning techniques above? And even if you can remember all of them, the when and how to use them in a sales call may be eluding you. Don't sweat it. You don't have to remember every type of question listed. In a later chapter, I plan to show you a specific questioning order that will be easy to remember!

So why did I even mention them? I mentioned them because I am trying to lay a foundation of questioning skills that will be helpful later in the PRECISE Actions. My objective is to get you to identify different questioning techniques in hope that you will use more questions than statements in your everyday communications. Who cares what order or what situation you use them? Who cares how many Little Yes vs. BWs you use? I don't. But to be PRECISE during a sales call, you need to make every word count. To make every word count you need to open them up.

> To get into your prospect's heads and hearts, get into the habit of asking questions.

Chapter Five

Listen Up!: If You Don't Have a Photographic Memory, Take Notes

Formula for Handling People
1. Listen to the other person's story.
2. Listen to the other person's full story.
3. Listen to the other person's full story first.
        —George C. Marshall (1880–1959), American military leader

I have seen dozens of average salespeople turn into good salespeople by evolving from statement pushers into expert questioners. But to become PRECISE, it is necessary to go even further by becoming an expert listener.

Now I know that you believe you have a damn good story to tell about your product or service. You are just dying to tell your prospect how great your solution is, but please be patient. As salespeople, we love to talk, but we need to resist the urge. Customers are often reluctant to talk, so it is important that we do everything we can to make them feel comfortable with the selling environment.

So ask questions that encourage your prospects to give the information that you need to customize your presentation. And when they are talking, listen up. They're trying to tell you how to sell them…they just don't know it. And don't tell your story too soon. Your time will come. Listen to their full story, and listen to their full story first. While they're expecting a smooth talker, you'll surprise the hell out of them by being a smooth listener. This will break down their defenses, but more important, get you the information you need to tell them what they want to hear.

It is like going fishing and having that big ol' bass tell you exactly what bait he will be biting on today. While the average angler chooses his bait based on assumptions, you choose yours based on the fish's input. But if you plan to ask the fish what he wants, you have to listen to what he tells you.

Question, Then Listen...Not Question, Then Think of Your Next Question

All of us do this, and it is a critical error in sales. Don't think about your next question until you listen to the answer to your last question. Too much information may be lost. One way to prevent this is by not asking questions that you don't want or need an answer to. Only ask questions that will bring about useful information. Don't just ask questions for the sake of asking questions. Ask questions that will benefit your customer and you. Ask questions that make you want to listen.

Have you ever been in a conversation with someone who asks you a question, and then doesn't listen to your response? And don't you just love that blank stare they give you like there is nobody home. You know these people. You can just tell that they have no interest in what you're saying and it drives you nuts. Or they give up the whole "eye contact" thing and begin looking around the room as if the answer to the question they just asked you is somewhere *out there.*

I have seen many sales representatives act this way with customers. It is as if they know they need to ask questions, but feel that they really don't need the information they requested, because they already know what the customer is going to say. I have seen this backfire on too many sales reps. They ask a question and then just keep going about their business as if they never even asked it. They shuffle paperwork, organize their product display, or just nod their heads as if they know exactly what the customer is going to say with a crinkled-up, "know-it-all" face. Don't do this. After asking a question, drop everything, and *just listen.*

> There is only one thing worse than not listening—
> it is asking a question and then not listening.

Now I know that customers will sometimes go off on a tangent in response to one of your questions, and you often feel like you have no choice but to fake that you care. Trust me, I don't blame you. But don't get into the habit of shutting down those active ears of yours. Once you turn them off, it is difficult to turn them back on. And while the customer is reciting the Gettysburg Address, there just might be a subliminal message in there telling you exactly what you should say to get that customer to buy your product. It would be a shame if you missed it because you shut down eight minutes ago.

> "A good listener is more than a good talker with a sore throat."
>
> —Anonymous

Salespeople that know how to effectively question their customers are already ahead of the pack. But to make it to the next level, they have to become even better at listening. You will become an expert questioner and an expert listener. And when you ask questions of your customer and it is time to listen, you will *actually* listen. Why? Because you will only ask questions that you want or need answers to.

Don't Fake It

There is yet another breed of sales listener. I call her the "Faker." She might even dress it up a little with that big "cheesy smile" or lean forward and put both hands on her cheeks like Arsenio Hall during an interview. But you just know that her mind is a million miles away, and she proves it when the response she gives the customer has nothing to do with what the customer just said. Hello!

Now there are quite a few fakers out there. In fact, I often have to slap myself for doing it. But I am not alone. I have seen many fine sales reps ask a question, fake like they are listening, and then go on with their story as if the customer never moved his lips. While these sales reps were off in La-La Land, all they were hearing from their customers was what Charlie Brown used to hear on the telephone when his grandmother would call (Waaa, Waaa, Waaaaaaaa...Waa Wa). The customer's lips are moving, but the sales rep hears nothing, and therefore misses critical clues that just might be needed.

Don't Interrupt

What's worse than carrying on a conversation with somebody who constantly interrupts you? You're in the middle of making your point and this bonehead feels the need to either dispute what you are saying or cut you off and finish your sentence for you. Ugh! When this happens, you lose interest in anything the "Interrupter" says. When a sales rep does this during a sales call, she not only risks having the prospect lose interest, she also risks ticking the prospect off. It doesn't matter how good your solution is if you have just alienated your prospect.

There are two reasons so many average sales reps interrupt their prospects:

1. They believe that projecting their thoughts and opinions is more important than learning about the customer's thoughts and opinions.

2. They feel that silence shows weakness.

We need to destroy these myths.

Myth #1—Projecting is More Important Than Learning

"A good listener is not only popular everywhere, but after awhile he knows something."

—Wilson Mizner (1876–1933), American playwright

While your thoughts and opinions are important in a sales call, they are not nearly as important as the thoughts and the opinions of your prospects. Before you ever meet with a prospect, you already know what you know. Do you believe that learning something from your prospect is important? If so, how much can you learn while you're talking? (Probably not a hell of a lot.) Remember that to be PRECISE means saying only what your customers want to hear. You cannot do this unless you know what your customers are thinking and feeling. So love their thoughts and opinions more than yours. If you do this, you will find that they will often love your thoughts and opinions even more than you do.

> Never talk just for the sake of talking—but always listen
> for the sake of learning.

Myth #2—Silence Shows Weakness

> "Under all speech that is good for anything there lies a silence that is better. Silence is deep as eternity; speech is shallow as time."
> —Thomas Carlyle (1795–1881), Scottish essayist and historian

Make silence part of your sales call. Silence shows strength, wisdom, and confidence. Some of the most influential people in history have used silence as a tool to stir action. Consider in silence everything your prospect says, and don't respond until you are sure that what you are going to say will be exact and sharply defined. While you are pondering your response, don't talk. Just think in silence until you feel confident that what you say next will be pure poetry.

Believe me, I understand just how difficult this can be. Silence for me used to be the equivalent of Chinese water torture. I hated any of it when I was selling. You see, I have a God-given ability to speak too much. I get so pumped in a sales call that I sometimes find myself making too many assumptions, too many statements, and feeling the need to fill every moment of silence with the painful sound of my own voice. Trust me, I can inflict pain when my sales game is not "on."

Silence:

• Prevents you from interrupting, and

• Prevents you from saying something you wish you hadn't.

Have you ever interrupted someone and said something that you wish you could take back two seconds after you said it? We all have. To prevent myself from interrupting the person I am speaking to and to prevent myself from saying something stupid, I have a quirky little system that makes it easier for me to let people finish what they are saying.

I wait until the person that I am speaking with completely finishes talking, and then I identify the last word he said. I then pause for a moment in silence and repeat that word in my mind. This exercise helps me focus on what the person is saying and forces me to listen until the very end. Then and only then am I allowed to think about what was said, work out my response, and then use the least amount of words possible to respond. This prevents me from interrupting people, and while on the job, prevents me from cutting off customers.

The same technique works when I am teaching sales. My classes are interactive, and I encourage involvement. Regardless of what industry or what part of the world I am teaching in, many of the same questions and areas of concern are expressed. My natural tendency is to jump in, head them off at the pass, and try to impress them with my mind reading abilities by responding to their questions or comments even before they finish. By trying to identify the very last word each person said, I am forced to let them finish their thoughts. And by taking a few seconds of silence before responding, I am forced to reflect on the meaning behind their words. This ensures that my response will be meaningful and PRECISE.

Practice with Family Members

The way we listen at home is even more important than the way we listen at work. Do you want to know if you are a good listener? Ask your husband, wife, brother, sister, mother, father, son, or daughter what they think. And when you ask them, focus on their response. Drop everything you are doing, look them in the eye, and listen to every word they say. And while they are telling you the way they feel, *don't interrupt them.* Let them finish talking, repeat their last word in your mind, and then take a few seconds to think about what they said. For this exercise, you need not respond when they are through. Just smile, maybe give them a little nod, and be done with it. You'll be amazed at how difficult it is to:

• Not interrupt.
• Listen until the very last word is spoken; and then identify that word.
• Use silence to help you think about what was said.

You'll also be impressed by how much you learned from their response.

How Good Is Your Memory?

After questioning and listening, your goal is to use the information your prospect shares with you. So a good memory must be useful and necessary during a sales call, right? Let's do a test to see how good your memory is.

Take a look at the pictures on Memory Test #1 for thirty seconds. Memorize as many of the pictures as you can. After you are finished, you will be asked to write down all the ones that you remember. Grab a watch and time yourself. Ready, set, go!

Memory Test #1

(Look for thirty seconds)

Okay, now that you are finished looking at the picture, cover it and write down what you saw in the space below.

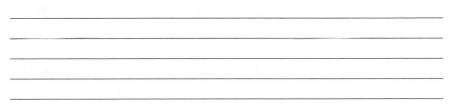

Now go back and compare. How many of the images did you remember—five, six, perhaps more? How difficult was it to remember them all? Now try Memory Test #2. Get that watch out and look at this image for thirty seconds. Try to remember as many phrases as possible. Go!

Memory Test #2
(Look for thirty seconds)

I want 2 day services

John Makes the decisions

Budget cycle ends in May

We like service contracts

Can you call Thursday?

We need at least 5

They are always on time

Sue and Jack will Be There

He takes a long time

Don't Be Late...EVER

Her B-day is Thursday

Okay, now cover the test and write down all the phrases that you can remember without looking back.

_____

_____

_____

_____

_____

Well, how did you do? Did you remember all of those phrases? If you did, then you have a great memory. If you didn't, then welcome to the world of the rest of us. Take a look at the previous test one more time. If all this information came out in one sales call would this be important information to know? Could this information help you be more PRECISE when presenting your solution? Would this information be helpful to know when preparing for follow-up calls? Would this information help you close the sale? *Of course!*

If you didn't get them all down, guess what? You don't have a photographic memory. So what! In sales, you don't have to. All you need is a working pen and a notepad. Now go back to Memory Test #2 once again and read the phrases out loud. As you are reading them, write them down.

When you finish, go back and compare what you wrote to the exact wording of the phrases on the test.

Can you believe it? They match identically. I know what you are saying. "No kidding, idiot, they are the same because I wrote them down as I looked at them. That's why I got them 100 percent correct."

Okay, if you like perfection, then do the same thing in a sales call. While they are giving you information, leave nothing to chance. Take everything down on a notepad. It will be these notes that will dictate your entire presentation.

Take Notes

In a sales call your notepad becomes your cheat sheet. When you take good notes, all the clues and the entire answer key are on that sheet of paper. Use the cheat sheet!

As I mentioned earlier in the book, I will never be mistaken for Albert Einstein. Luckily for me, I knew this at an early age so I was able to compensate for it over the years. It hit me at the age of nine while playing a game called "Simon" with the smart kid in the neighborhood named Bill Derwin. Simon was a game that consisted of four large different-colored buttons that light up, each making a different sound when they did. Simon would spit out a sequence of lights and sounds, and it was the person playing the game's responsibility to press the buttons in the same order that Simon produced them. Billy D., as I fondly called him, was an expert at this game and could remember and repeat a sequence that consisted of a dozen or more lights and beeps. His memory was amazing; mine was not.

So what's the point? My point is, unless you have a memory like Billy D., take a notepad into your call. When your customer starts spewing a bunch of "sounds and colors," write them down on your notepad. When it is time for you to use that information to customize your presentation, it won't sound like you are an alien. If I only took notes while playing that Simon game, I just might have been able to keep up with Billy D.

Doesn't a Notepad Take the Focus Off My Customer?

I get this every time I teach PRECISE Selling. The usual response is, "I don't like to take notes because I don't want to bury my head in a notepad. I like to look at my customers while I'm selling to them." Of course, this response is usually preceded or followed by the standard, "I have been selling for a lot of years and…"

Anyway, I do understand that it might seem like a contradiction to say that you have to be completely focused on customers and what they're saying and at the same time be taking notes on what they're saying. With this being the case, there is a right way and a wrong way to take notes. The rule of thumb is to jot down only the information that reveals what is in the customer's head and heart. It will be these notes that will become the outline of your presentation. So take only as many as you will need to keep you PRECISE…no more, no less. As mentioned earlier, I am no Billy D., so I tend to write a few more than others. But it's important for you to understand that if you are not used to taking notes, it will feel like the call has come to a stand still while your pen is moving. Don't worry. The benefits of having the information on that pad will outweigh any negatives that you may be concerned about. And it doesn't matter how big or how small your notepad is, it's all in how you use it. In short, just make sure that you have something large enough to fit all the information that your prospect is giving you. If you ask a Barbara Walters question of someone, and they begin telling you things like:

- What company they used in the past
- What they liked about that company
- What they've hated about that company
- How much they're willing to spend
- Who makes the decisions
- The decision-making time frame
- The key decision-maker's names
- What they had for dinner last night
- Their birthday and favorite hobby

…and you don't have a pen and a notepad handy, I have two words for you…*you're dead.*

I have seen this happen countless times. It is at this point the sales rep should swallow her pride and ask permission to reach into her briefcase so she can take notes that will help her better serve her customer.

Of course, there are others that decide to ride out the storm and pull the patented "faker" technique. These salespeople just shake their heads, act like they can remember everything the prospect is saying, and then launch into their canned presentation that they planned on giving anyway. And in the process they waste many words and much time.

Do Customers Want You to Take Notes?

Have you ever been to a restaurant and had the waiter come up to you to take your order without a pen and paper? Sure, we all have. How did it make you feel when the person you were with began making special requests? Or perhaps you are one of those people. You know, "Hold the mayo…add some onions…I'd like it medium-rare…no, wait, I mean medium-well…and can you bring that out at the same time as my appetizer?" While this behavior might annoy the average person, it is no doubt the right of the customer to ask for something that she would be totally satisfied with. Is it too much for the customer to expect the order to be delivered accurately? Of course not!

I don't care if that non-notetaking waiter is in the Restaurant Hall of Fame and is renowned for his food memory skills. For the twenty minutes that I'm waiting for that food, I'm stressed out about whether he is going to screw it up. The only way I will be able to sit back and enjoy that glass of wine while I wait is to know the waiter understands exactly what I want and has every aim of getting it right. If what I want does not find its way onto that sheet of paper, the chances of that waiter delivering perfection are lessened. So if you don't want to "stress out" your customers, and if you want to deliver PRECISE perfection, all it takes is an investment in the notepad of your choice and a reliable pen.

Wrap-Up

While the basic principles of listening and taking notes as discussed in this chapter seem like common sense, these are two skills that do not come naturally for many of us. We like being the "star" of the sales show and enjoy the feeling of total control in the call. But it is by forcing ourselves to listen—I mean truly listen—that we can reveal our true intent: to provide the customer with a "five-star" selling experience. And by forcing ourselves to take notes, we show our customers that we care enough about what they say to make sure we pay attention to every detail they give us. Do these two things well, and you will display a "sales selflessness" that will separate you from the pack. So on your next call, be sure to carry two big ears, two working pens, and the notepad of your choice. These are the essential weapons of a PRECISE Selling top performer, and that's what you are about to become.

PART TWO
THE THREE PS OF THE
PRECISE SELLING FORMULA

So far we have laid a foundation of effective sales communication. We discussed the importance of minimizing statements, asking PRECISE questions, sharply listening, and taking notes. We are now entering the real "meat" of PRECISE Selling.

Posture, PIC Knowledge, and PRECISE Actions are the bedrock of PRECISE Selling. These three simple elements are what separate the true pro from the average Joe hitting the pavement or phones everyday. As a sales professional, difficult challenges and tasks ranging from menial to three-alarm-fire are bombarding you everyday. And if you are like most, you sometimes feel like you have lost complete control over your own destiny. Your territory and your customers own you and sometimes you do well serving them, and sometimes you fall short. Sometimes you even feel like you are doing a great job only to find out that you still managed to tick somebody off. Other times you feel like you may not be doing everything necessary, your confidence is down and—boom, in comes that big order that you thought would never go through. In fact, sometimes your best orders occur when you are on vacation. Figure that one out.

While I admit that it sometimes feels like everything just happens by chance, I am here to tell you that if you simply key in on the fundamentals that I am about to teach you, you will be better than 99 percent of all sales reps that you compete against. It does not matter what industry you are in or what products or services you sell. If you constantly think about the three Ps and put them into action in your lives, you will be your company's top performer. And it will happen in 20 days or less.

PRECISE Selling Formula of Top Performers

1) **P**osture

2) **P**IC Knowledge
- Product
- Industry
- Competition

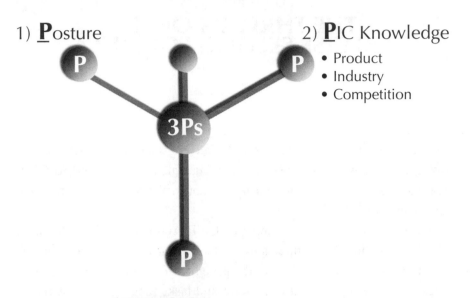

3) **PRECISE** Actions

P #1—PRECISE Posture: How to Get Your Customers, Colleagues, and CEO to Want to Be Just Like You

Main Entry: 'pos·ture
Function: noun
1: the position or bearing of the body whether characteristic or assumed for a special purpose

How often have you heard the expression "she carries herself very well"? When people say this, they are talking about posture—the position or bearing of the body, whether characteristic or assumed. Why is this so important when in front of a customer? Well, the way you manage your own body can tell a customer a lot about how you will manage their business.

Why is the Position or Bearing of Your Body Important?

I like to use teenagers as an example. Unfortunately, there is a social World War III going on between style and posture throughout high schools and universities. In fact, proper—or PRECISE—posture seems to be losing the battle in a large way. If you are curious about what I mean, go ahead and walk over to your television set and turn it on. Grab that remote and change the channel to MTV and watch for about ninety seconds.

Okay, I know I should be more open to individual expression, but you will have to excuse me for thinking the guy with the pink hair, pants falling off, and body slouched over is not somebody who I would say has

PRECISE Posture. While this posture might get him a few chest bumps and high-fives from strangers at a concert, when it comes to trusting that person to handle any business that I might consider important, well… While this might be an extreme example of poor posture, the truth remains that people will form an opinion about others within the first seven seconds of any meeting.

PRECISE Posture Tells Them That You Are Capable

Main Entry: 'pos·ture
Function: noun
2: state or condition at a given time, especially with respect to capability in particular circumstances

Rudy Giuliani had a challenge on that horrible day, September 11, 2001. New York City, and in fact, the entire country, was looking to the mayor for guidance. The stakes could not be higher as everyone around the world was watching to see how the city's leader would respond to the tragedy that had just unfolded. Rudy's posture was nothing short of remarkable. Look at the definition above and tell me what Rudy's state or condition was with respect to his capability in that particular circumstance. His actions and reactions to what just happened had a direct impact on the mental state of the people that were watching.

George Bush stood on the rubble of Ground Zero with his arm around a firefighter and with confidence, assured the rescue workers and the world the U.S. would avenge this horrific act. Regardless of your political affiliation, there was little doubt the posture of both Rudy and George gave peace of mind to millions of people. Had their posture been anything short of PRECISE, millions of Americans would have been adversely affected. It was their posture that gave Americans the confidence and the ability to begin to pick up the pieces and rebuild.

- PRECISE Posture breeds confidence
- PRECISE Posture gives peace of mind
- PRECISE Posture destroys fear
- PRECISE Posture breaks down barriers
- PRECISE Posture encourages others to open up

PRECISE Posture is a way of carrying yourself that tells your customers that you are capable of making their lives better somehow. A salesperson that carries PRECISE posture is a "spark." She is somebody that makes things happen, breeds confidence, gives peace of mind, destroys fear, breaks down barriers, and encourages others to open up. This "spark" has a unique ability to ask the right questions, listen effectively, sift through the rubble and relay solutions as Rudy and George Bush did so wonderfully after 9/11. This catalyst has the ability to transfer that confidence to his customers and achieve results in the end. To do these things, to be a catalyst, you need to have PRECISE Posture.

How Does Attitude Affect Your Posture?

Main Entry: 'pos·ture
3: a conscious mental or outward behavioral attitude

Attitude is the foundation of a PRECISE Posture. It is the fuel to the salesperson's body and mind, and it sets his compass in one of many directions. While a positive attitude does not guarantee sales success, it does assure many things. It assures that you can face rejection and overcome countless obstacles that are unavoidable in sales. There will be times in this business when "the worst" happens. When those days come, when you are experiencing the worst, don't make the worst of it.

> If you think you are beaten, you are.
> If you think you dare not, you don't!
> If you want to win, but think you can't, it's almost a cinch you won't.
> If you think you'll lose, you've lost.
> For out in the world we find success begins with a fellow's will; it's all in the state of the mind. Life's battles don't always go to the stronger and faster man, but sooner or later the man who wins is the man who thinks he can.
> —Walter D. Wintle

Pessimism Will Kill You

Pessimistic attitudes are like a disease. According to the ASPS (American Society of Pessimistic Salespeople) it affects nearly four of five salespeople. Unfortunately, it afflicts most salespeople who have been selling for three years or more and the condition often worsens with time. For you salespeople who find yourselves afflicted with this disease, please keep it to yourself. It is highly contagious and can make many people around you sick to their stomachs. And frankly, it just plain stinks.

This Room Stinks

> One Sunday afternoon, a cranky grandfather was visiting his family. As he laid down to take a nap, his grandson decided to have a little fun by putting Limburger cheese on his grandfather's mustache. Soon, grandpa awoke with a snort and charged out of the bedroom saying, "This room stinks." Through the house he went, finding every room smelling the same. Desperately, he made his way outside, only to find that "the whole world stinks!"

When we fill our brains with pessimistic thoughts, everything we experience and every selling situation we come upon will carry an odor.

How Does Enthusiasm Affect Your Posture?

> "If you aren't fired with enthusiasm, you will be *fired* with enthusiasm."
> —Vince Lombardi (1913–1970), professional football coach

Well, don't go getting fired from your job. If being enthusiastic is what it takes to keep your job, then do it. Truth is, you're either excited about what you are selling or you are not. While buyers do not have to show elation as they become more interested in your product, you do. You cannot expect your customer to show buying signals if you don't even show them yourself. I often hear salespeople tell me that their personality will not allow them to show much emotion, and that they are just not emotional people.

Well, I am not asking you to do back flips or jump around like you just won the Powerball. I am, however, telling you that product information alone is often not enough to spark buying emotions in your customer. Your emotion is often the only tool to stir your prospect's interest and involvement in what you are selling.

> To get enthusiasm, you need to give enthusiasm.

So You're Stingy with Enthusiasm

Bill Parcells, current coach of the Dallas Cowboys, and former coach of the New York Jets, New England Patriots, and New York Giants, has never been known to show much positive emotion. So when one of his players walks off the field and gets anything close to a grin for something he did, that player knows he is excited.

If you would consider yourself more like a Bill Parcells, then maybe your emotional outburst is to just smile for 4.2 seconds when you mention a benefit of your product. If you are traditionally a mope, and your prospect is an existing customer and knows this, then that 4.2 seconds might just convince her that you do actually like what you are selling. In any case, throw a little zeal, as much as you can spare, into your presentation. More customers will buy from you based on your passion for your product or service than for any other reason.

> "He had a winning smile, but everything else was a loser."
>
> —George C. Scott

Customers can see right through a cheesy smile that lacks sincerity. While many people believe that salespeople should be smiling all the time, there are times while you are in front of your customer when a smile just does not make sense.

After working for several months to penetrate a large clinic system in Chicago, I was finally able to get an appointment with a key equipment decision maker. During that visit I discovered that they were dissatisfied with the product performance and the follow-up service that they had been getting from their current supplier, who was our biggest competitor. Switching to my company's products would also be a bit painful, as it would cost a considerable sum of money and time. But this was a move they were prepared to make. While the whole process was tormenting but necessary for them, it was sheer ecstasy for me.

This is a perfect example of a time when it would have been a bit inappropriate for me to sit there with a big smile on my face. A winning smile, on that occasion, would have turned me into a big loser, and that was a sale I refused to lose.

Smiles come in many shapes and sizes. When the situation calls for it, you need to reach into your bag of smiles and find the perfect one. Think of what emotion you are trying to stir up or sustain with that customer, and that's the one you want to use. If, in your heart, you believe the benefits of your product or service will provide so much value and happiness, go ahead and slap on a big one. If you sell replacement parts for broken furnaces, and the Sullivan Family just called and needs your sales or service expertise in a hurry, it might be best just to keep the big grin in your back pocket.

Body Language: Monkey See, Monkey Do

Many sales books talk about the importance of being able to read body language during a sales call, and this is no doubt an important part of selling. However, you as a salesperson have some control over what body language your customer is speaking.

Several years ago I was in Barcelona, Spain, doing some sightseeing, and my friend and I decided to go to the zoo. Now, I am not sure what your favorite part of the animal kingdom is, but for me it is the primate section. Monkeys and apes just crack me up, and this day was no exception. While my friend was off at the restroom, I casually strolled over to the area where the monkeys were. Now I know nothing about monkeys and apes but if you have ever been to the zoo, you know that monkeys are like salespeople. You have your lazy mopes that just lie around picking bugs out of their hair. You have others that run from tree to tree indiscriminately (time management problems) with no focus. You have the ones that seem content with what is going on that will occasionally pick up a stick and smack something around. And then you have the ones that are just plain hilarious. In fact, I think these are funnier than 95 percent of the actors getting paid the big bucks doing sitcoms.

This day was no different. As I pressed my face up against the glass to get a better look, one "funny" monkey approached the glass from his side and looked right into my eyes. I looked over my shoulder to see if anybody was watching, then I turned back around and gave the monkey a comical face. (You know, the kind of face you sometimes make in the hotel mirror for no apparent reason.) After I curled my lips up and stuck my tongue out I watched as the monkey not only did what I did, he topped me. Let me tell you, Jim Carrey had nothing on that monkey. He could do things with his face that I had never seen. I then completely lost it. I curled my arms into a Hulk-like pose and continued to scratch my armpits while blurting out the traditional monkey call…EEE, EEE, EEE. Now, I had never actually seen a monkey do this, but I know as a kid I did it all the time, so I had to have picked it up from some credible source. Well, this monkey followed my lead and began scratching under his armpits. There was a definite game of "Monkey See, Monkey Do" going on here.

This little exercise continued for about two minutes until I grew uncomfortable with where my new monkey friend began scratching himself. Just as I turned around, there was an elderly woman that had obviously been watching me doing my thing, and what a moment that was. I not only felt embarrassed about what I was doing, I felt like my grandmother just caught me playing with the neighborhood problem child.

What is my point? We project our body language and facial expressions onto our customers. While I do not feel comfortable comparing your customers to monkeys, I will. If you find yourself eye to eye with the monkey, be aware that the language your body and mouth are speaking will have an effect on how that monkey reacts. If you show little excitement about your product or service, your customer will show little excitement. If your lip curls up and your eyebrows drop down because you are confused about your product, your customer will appear confused. If you shrug your shoulders because you cannot answer your customer's question, your customer will shrug her shoulders when you ask for the order.

Project positive body and facial language and your customer will follow.

Turn the Lights on When You Dress

Dressing for success might be simple for some, but for me it has always been a challenge. I am not what you would call "fashion forward." In fact, if my wife would allow me to sleep in khakis and a polo shirt I would be just fine with it. Luckily this lack of style has not seemed to affect my ability to sell and sell often.

Perhaps my biggest "blunder" occurred in 1992 when I was new to my Chicago territory. I had been trying to get an appointment with the CEO of one of our biggest distribution customers with little success.

Then one day I broke the code and the bigwig's secretary had agreed, with his permission, to get me in the appointment book. My objective was to introduce myself and see what I could do to get this company's sales force to sell more of my product instead of the competitor's. Don was a big name in the industry and had a long relationship with the officers in my company. I was a bit intimidated and felt like I was in over my head.

As Don entered the room, I put on my early version of a PRECISE Posture. I may not have convinced him at the time, but I was feeling like a CEO that day, and I was sure to convince him that I was a seasoned professional. The conversation was going great and Don had just agreed to run a promotion with some of my focus products when the wheels fell off. While we were having our little chat, Don took on a casual demeanor and crossed his legs.

Minutes later, feeling cozy with the situation, I did the same. As I pulled my foot up to casually cross it across my knee, I could not help but to admire my shiny black, winged-tip shoe. Man, had I arrived! As the meeting progressed I was feeling invincible. It was now time to readjust this "smooth as hell" posture of mine, so I lifted my winged-tip, and the right foot that was wearing it, off of my left knee. As I pulled up my left foot to rest it on my other knee I saw one of the scariest things I had seen in my professional career.

On my opposite foot I was not wearing that fancy black winged-tip, but instead was sporting a handsome maroon tasseled loafer. That's right, I had done the unthinkable. I had walked out of the house with two different shoes on. Not only were they different shoes, but one was a slip-on and the other one I would have had to tie.

What was I to do? Well, I had little choice but to slowly look up at Don, let him finish his sentence and then confess. I said, "Don, I need to show you something and this might change everything." I had no choice but to laugh at the situation. As I stood up and showed him, I did a little Irish jig with my feet and he just about fell over laughing. He lost it even more when I told him I had a pair just like it at home. From that day forward, Don was my best customer. It was my fashion misstatement that solidified the relationship and provided laughs at meetings for years.

> "When I see a man of shallow understanding extravagantly clothed, I feel sorry—for the clothes."
>
> —Josh Billings

While I do not recommend that you go out of the house with two different shoes on, I do recommend that you be yourself as it relates to fashion. Some of the most successful people in the business world have made it without the two-thousand-dollar Italian suit and Rolex watch. Warren Buffet, king of the business and investment world, is one such example. He impresses with who he is and what he knows, not with what he wears. While I don't mean to suggest there is a downside to being the best dressed at the sales meeting, I do mean to suggest that it will not make or break you in the world of sales.

> It's not the suit—it's what's holding it up.

How to Make Your Customers Want to Be You

There are just some people who command the attention and respect of others. These people often have an unidentifiable charismatic posture about them that people are magnetically attracted to. I have seen customers wallow over sales reps that had PRECISE Posture. It's fun to watch. They laugh at every joke, compliment every new tie, and offer to fix them up with their most respected family member.

PRECISE Posture can make up for several things. I have seen some excellent salespeople with limited PIC Knowledge influence their customers based solely on the respect and trust that they have earned. When a salesperson carries herself with PRECISE Posture, people want to be around her, people want to hear what she says, and people want to do business with her. Why? Because as the cliché goes, "Sales is still a relationship business." It's about friendships. It's about an authenticity that tells the customer that, while we both have a job to do (I'm selling and you're buying), it's still important that we enjoy the encounter. So while a PRECISE Posture is about bringing the defenses down, it is also about allowing both you and your customer to enjoy the ride.

Chapter Seven
How a "Stupid" Posture Can Mean Big Money

Okay, I'm sick of fighting it. I can't hide anymore. I am a stupid salesperson! Go ahead…say it with me. Louder! We are having an old-fashioned comin' out party. For years we have been ashamed of who we are. Hell, most of us won't even admit that we are salespeople anymore. Over the years, a bunch of cute new titles have sprung up to replace "salesperson." We have hidden behind the vale of such milk-toast titles as:

Sales Associate

Hope: "They will look at me more as a pal!" Associate does mean buddy, chum, comate, companion, comrade, crony, pal, running mate, friend (at least according to Webster).

Truth: We are not their friends. When was the last time a sales associate called you on the phone or knocked on your door and you said, "Damn, I am dying to associate with you"?

Solutions Consultant

Hope: "Consultants give advice. That's why I do what I do. I give good advice."

Truth: Regardless of what we say, everybody knows our goal. Here's some advice: we must stop advising and start selling.

Service Agent

Hope: "They'll think I am the James Bond of sales."

Truth: There is nothing undercover about what we do. We have been exposed. They know why we have come…for their money.

Account Manager

Hope: "My prospects respect me more. They just might think I'm high on the corporate ladder. You know…manager and all."

Truth: Why on earth do we want to be managers? They make less than us and have to deal with a bunch of menial garbage. They can have the title; we'll take the cash.

Relationship Manager

Hope: "They will know that my relationships mean more than my sales numbers."

Truth: We are not working for a dating service. And our relationship with our husband, wife, or significant other will improve if we bring home more bacon. Who's more important?

We must get over it! The sooner we go to that mirror, put our game face on, and say, "I am a stupid salesperson. I make my living selling," the sooner we will be able to take back that badge of honor that so many cheesy salespeople have ruined.

And once we are proud of who we are and what we do, we can then take it to the next level. And what a blast that next level can be. It's time to be stupid. Only this stupid is not the stupid that makes your prospects want to avoid you. This stupid is one that makes them want to be with you, act like you, and buy from you. And although sometimes difficult, this stupid puts more money in your commission check than it is used to.

Now that we have all admitted who we are, we will now get on with the business of separating ourselves from the "I am not a salesperson" crowd. Now I know this can be a difficult task. In fact, in the United States, there are over thirty-four million salespeople. In the medical sales field, where I began my career, there are over ninety thousand salespeople trying to get the attention of customers. Think about it! How many salespeople serve your industry? Well, guess what. When prospects have that many people calling on them, they begin to go numb. With such a barrage of average and below-average sales performers hounding our customers daily, it makes it harder than ever for us to separate ourselves from them. Nevertheless, to increase the number of customer contacts we make and to make each one more valuable, *we must stand out, we must get noticed.*

So while the Solutions Consultants and Account Managers are busy hiding, doing everything they can to *not* get noticed, you, with your professional yet stupid PRECISE Posture, will be highly visible. "Stupid?" you say. Yes, "stupid!" The definition of a "stupid salesperson" in my world is a "creative and calculated risk-taker." So let's discuss why it's so important.

Being Stupid Can Brighten People's Day...Including Yours

I know this is the part in the book where I am supposed to tell you about the impact just one individual can have on everyone around them. And how a smile and a sunshiny demeanor are infectious, contagious, and communicable. I can hear it now, "If I can touch just one customer today and spread some happiness, my day will be worthwhile." Hey, if that motivates you, go nutty. But as an occasional self-centered mope who has never been mistaken for Tony Robbins, I am a different kind of motivator. This selfish motivator tells you:

You have to, need to, and must separate yourself from all other sales people. If you do, you will sell more, make more money, and your days will be brighter than ever. If you choose to not stand out because that is "just not you," then you must be prepared to melt into the lonely but crowded world of the unnoticed. If you go unnoticed, your pay increases will go unnoticed as well.

Ask yourself how many customers really noticed you after every day's work. And I am not talking about the "Of course they noticed. I called on them and they spoke to me," type of notice. I am talking about the "they smiled, laughed, were surprised, were excited, and were noticeably thankful" notice. This notice only comes when you add a spark to an otherwise routine sales call.

> "I would rather be ashes than dust! I would rather that my spark should burn out in a brilliant blaze than it should be stifled by dry-rot. I would rather be a superb meteor, every atom of me in magnificent glow, than a sleepy and permanent planet. The proper function of man is to live, not to exist. I shall not waste my days in trying to prolong them. I shall use my time."
>
> —Jack London (1876–1916), American writer
> *London reportedly spoke these words to his friends*
> *two months before he died at the age of thirty-nine.*

Levels of Stupidity

There are different levels of stupidity, and it is up to you decide what your *stupidity tolerance* is.

Modestly Stupid

Some salespeople just don't feel comfortable standing out in a stupid way. They believe the way they service their customers distinguishes them enough. If this is how you feel, then no problem. But don't think I am going to let you off that easy. There are subtle ways to distinguish yourself that do not require you to put on a gorilla suit. While standing out is important, it also has to suit your comfort level and personality.

Here are some modestly stupid methods to get noticed and stay noticed:

Thank-You Notes

Write short, handwritten thank-you notes. This is a quick and easy—yet effective—way to get noticed. And make writing these notes a habit. If you are in outside sales, perhaps driving around in that fancy Ford Taurus, keep a stack of thank-you notes and stamps with you. After your call, take thirty seconds to write a few words like:

Dear Michelle,
I wanted to drop you a note to thank you for the opportunity to meet with you today. I hope our solution is what you were looking for. If not, thanks anyway for giving us a look. I will follow up next Tuesday. In the meantime, have a great week!
Thanks again—Brian

Today's sales world has become impersonal. So, to get the greatest impact from your note, make sure it is in your handwriting and not your computer's. (I know, I used a computer in my example, but you will have to give me a mulligan on this one.) Your handwriting shows that you care enough about your customers to take a few extra minutes to recognize their importance to you.

Immediately after writing your note, put a stamp on the envelope and find the nearest mailbox. When your customer gets that note one or two days later, they will be impressed with your follow-up, and it will give them a small hint of your attention to detail. I have been doing this for many years now, and it is almost comical how much business it has earned me. I have had dozens of prospects tell me that a little note or card meant the difference between getting the business and not.

If you do most of your selling over the phone, this tactic also works well. In fact, a thank-you note with a picture of yourself will help your prospect better relate to you. Many customers have been serviced by the same phone salesperson for years without ever even knowing what the rep even looked like. Send a picture of you and your family. They will get a better understanding of who you are, and this will help strengthen your relationship.

These thank-you notes and spontaneous cards work in other areas as well. In fact, one of these stupid little notes helped me "win" my dream home.

The Thirty-Year Card

It feels great to win a sale, but it feels even better to "win" the home that you plan to live in for the next thirty years. Let me explain. Only recently my wife and I found our dream home. This red brick colonial was the home that we had talked about for many years, so when it came on the market we jumped at the chance to put in an offer. After doing so, our realtor told us the sellers accepted our offer. We were elated, and immediately began planning our move.

Three hours after receiving the phone call of the seller's acceptance, our realtor called to say there was a problem. She said that another couple had put in an offer before us and that they were under the assumption that it had been accepted. While they had nothing in writing, they said they had a verbal acceptance and that, by law, was sufficient. This caused some confusion between all parties, and nobody knew what to do. Personally, I felt like I had just been kicked in the chest.

After several discussions, it was determined that rather than have this disagreement handled by the courts, instead both potential buyers would resubmit a closed bid. These bids would be hand-delivered by the realtors, and the sellers would choose one family at their kitchen table at nine o'clock that evening. This, my friends, was looking a lot like an eBay house auction. At this point, I had no idea what price to go in at, I just knew that I wanted that house. The game was on!

While discussing the price, my realtor surprised the hell out of me and became totally stupid. She reminded me of the value of stupid little cards and recommended that I write one that she could deliver with the new bid. ("Why didn't I think of that myself?" I thought.) I sat on my computer and pulled a picture of the house off the Internet. I combined that house shot with a sappy picture of my family, wrote the most purely PRECISE, hand-written, brown-nosed, groveling material that I could think of, and dropped it in an envelope.

At 10:30 that night, the sellers had chosen us. Their realtor told us that although both bids were close (which to me meant the other buyer's bid was higher), they chose to go with us because, "Mrs. Knight loved that card. She said she was going to take it to school tomorrow to show her students." When she told us this, I almost fell over.

My family will probably spend the next three decades in this house while sharing countless memories. That's a lot of Thanksgivings and Christmases. Isn't it amazing the impact that this little card may have on the next thirty years of our lives? Maybe I'm overanalyzing that card's importance, but I don't think so. The point is: stupid little things like thank-you notes and cards can have a huge impact. Make them a tool for stupid success in your professional *and* personal life.

Newsletters
A great way to keep your visibility up is with a newsletter. They are effective if you have an existing customer base, be it in person or over the phone. In your newsletter, tell success stories about your products or services and include testimonials from happy users. Take a picture of your happy customers and slap their attractive mugs on the front cover (get their permission first, of course). They will love the attention you are giving them and other customers will want to be part of future newsletters.

Moderately Stupid
If you find yourself able to go beyond the previous examples, you may want to consider the following moderately stupid techniques.

Voice Mail Commercials

Let's face it. We hate voice mail. That being said, it is an essential part of business communications. This does not mean that voice mail has to be dull. On the contrary, a thirty-second outbound greeting delivered to customers leaving you a message might be just enough to make somebody's day. So what do you say? One stupid fellow named John Moran, who I will discuss in more detail later, is famous for using different days in the calendar to entertain his customers. In fact, at this moment, I will stop typing and dial John's number. Please hold, a representative will be with you shortly...

(three minutes later)

Okay, I'm back. After dialing John's number, I found myself laughing as I learned from John's outbound message a few short but interesting facts about the great composer Beethoven. In fact, according to the message, today is Beethoven's birthday. I am still not sure if John realizes that Beethoven was not responsible for the song, "Roll Over Beethoven" that played in the background of his message.

While a message such as this might seem strange, it is effective in distinguishing John from others. In fact, I can think of few Senior VPs of Sales of major corporations that pride themselves as much as John on the art of stupidity. It is this stupidity that causes customers to go out of their way to do business with John. He makes the mundane fun and creates and solidifies countless relationships while doing so.

Magnets

If you agree that visibility is important, then make yourself visible when you are not even with your customers. An effective way of doing this is by creating magnets with your picture on them. On the magnet, put a fun slogan that will make them laugh and also makes a point about how well you will service them; or perhaps how bad you want their business. One of my favorites had a picture of the salesperson with the quote underneath from a song by a band called The Spinners. It said,

"Whenever you call me I'll be there
Whenever you want me I'll be there
Whenever you need me I'll be there
I'll be around...."

This is good stuff. And this sales rep put these magnets up around the offices and hid them in areas where customers would find them later. While some salespeople might believe this is overdoing it, this sales rep surprised his customers and amused them as they stumbled on the magnets stuck inside cabinets, refrigerators, and even attached to car doors. Of course, before taking it to this extreme, make sure that you have an established relationship. Regardless, this is a simple way to stand out. While others drop off a tiresome business card that gets buried among a hundred others, yours will grab your customer's attention. And who knows, it might even brighten up their day a bit.

Totally Stupid

Being totally stupid takes a little risk, but the potential benefits can build the foundation of the most loyal customers. Here are some of the most stupid examples I have witnessed.

In the medical industry there is a company called Midmark that does a fantastic job of being stupid. In fact, their totally stupid former sales leader, Scott Fanning, helped to create a culture of complete stupidity that spread like a disease throughout the company. This "fun and creative" culture has made the company famous in the industry and highly visible to their distribution partners. Midmark, like other medical manufacturers, relies heavily on its distribution salespeople to do much of the prospecting and selling. While these salespeople are an extension of the Midmark sales force, they are still "customers." Because these distributors have thousands of products to sell from hundreds of manufacturers, it is difficult for them to decide which product to promote when in front of a physician. So it is the job of the manufacturers to try to steal the mindshare of these distributors by remaining highly visible. With this visibility as a main objective, Midmark does everything it can to make sure that its company and its products are in a prominent place in the distribution reps minds always.

An example of this was illustrated during a year-end industry convention. Midmark made half their sales force dress up in tuxedos and the other half dress up in wedding gowns. This might not seem that stupid except there were no women dressed in wedding gowns. All the "brides" were men that weighed an average of 220 pounds. Their theme for that meeting was, "We Are Married to Our Distributors," and it was a huge hit. Their distribution customers still talk about this. And it didn't stop there. Many sales reps, long after the meeting was over, would show up at the front door of these distributors on a standard workday, all decked out in the same wedding dress. Want to add spice to a typical workday? Try this one. They will never forget you.

Another one of my favorites comes from the same company. The objective for one sales meeting was to convince the distributor reps how easy it was to demonstrate the Midmark product to physicians. If they could prove how easy it was to demonstrate, perhaps the distribution sales-people would spend more time focusing on it instead of something else.

To make their point, they themed the meeting, "It Is So Easy, a Monkey Could Sell It." Their product was a doctor's office exam room table. Well, in sticking with the theme, they actually trained a monkey how to do some parts of the exam table demonstration. During the meeting, a monkey walked through the door dressed in a suit and carrying a briefcase. After setting a briefcase down, he began pulling out drawers, pressing buttons, and pointing to different features, all along showing incredible enthusiasm for his product. The distribution salespeople absolutely lost it when they saw this. Is this something that you would easily forget? I wouldn't.

Another one of my favorites deals with a fictional character called Dr. Ben Dover, Proctologist. Dr. Ben is Welch Allyn Inc.'s national accounts salesperson, Tony Melaro. Ten years ago, Tony created a nerdy doctor character that wears a bright yellow coat, glasses with tape on it, and proctology instruments filling every pocket. On those days when he walks into his customer's offices dressed as the famous proctologist, handing out Dr. Ben buttons, T-shirts, golf balls, and now bobble-head dolls, the work-place lights up. He makes everybody's day and in the process, builds a fortress around his relationship. He is now stupidly famous in the indus-try and the competition can't touch his business. In fact, I often use Dr. Ben's talents in my PRECISE Selling seminars, and his character never disappoints.

I could write an entire book consisting of stupid stories like this. In each case, the stupid person or company took what many consider a risk, but every one of these risks paid off. While the competition was saying, "I won't act stupid," stupidly postured salespeople were counting their com-mission dollars and having a blast doing it.

Identify Your Stupidity Tolerance...Then Be "Stupider!"

Many salespeople sell products or services that are difficult to differentiate from the competition. Your customers can often pick up the phone or go online and order a similar solution for a few dollars less or a few dollars more. So how do you give yourself an edge over your competitors? I have three letters for you...Y-O-U. You are it, my friend. So if nothing about your product, service, or company separates you, it is your uniqueness that can.

You are a big feature and benefit that comes free with your product or service. What a bonus! So strut your stuff. Sell yourself. Commit to standing out. Start by finding a stupidity that you feel comfortable with, and work to become more stupid each month. Remember, the benefits of this behavior can be selfish; that's okay. Whatever motivates you—the attention you get, the extra money you earn, or the happiness you spread—who cares? Just know there are so few negatives to this behavior. And don't feel like you have to be stupid everyday. Even Don Rickles took a day off now and then. Perhaps you just pick one day to be stupid. But when you do, make that stupid day a habit.

People like their leisure time more than they like their work time, with a few exceptions. Hell, they built a restaurant chain based on the famous cliché "TGIF." Well, forget Friday! I like to be stupid on Tuesday. I call it TGIT—Thank God It's Tuesday! Why Tuesday? Because Tuesday gets a bum wrap.

Today, I am making a proclamation. Tuesday is officially PRECISE Selling's Stupid Day. This is the day when you should focus at least 72 percent of your energy on making everyone's day around you brighter and more fun by being stupid. And why are you doing this? You're doing it to sell more stuff and make more stupid money.

Okay, I really don't care what day you pick, but do try to pick a day to stand out. If you make it a habit, you will look forward to it, plan for it, and actually do it. And I guarantee you that your job will be a hell of a lot more fun than you ever thought it could be.

The Day I "Stupidly" Walked Outside the Lines

I just walked off a plane from Sioux Falls, South Dakota, and landed in terminal one of Chicago's O'Hare airport. I was tired, greasy, and couldn't wait to get to my cozy town home and plop myself down on my slightly weathered leather couch. As I walked through the crowd, I was stopped dead in my tracks by one of Chicago's finest. This police officer held his hands roughly two inches from my nose and said in his Chicago brogue, "Excuse me, sir, you can't go any further. I'm going to need you to stop right there, look down at those two white lines taped on the floor, and follow them directly to the left, where all the other people are following." As I began to question him, he quickly silenced me with a "Hey, buddy, enough of the lip…now move it along."

Like a cow following the herd, I took a few steps but quickly realized there were people that were "outside the lines" and were, in fact, walking behind the officer in the "forbidden" zone. At that point, I had to make a decision. I could follow the "cows" and stay between the lines, or take a little risk and follow the wild pack. So I took a step over that line and began walking with the others. After about twenty yards, I heard someone yell, but it wasn't "Hey buddy, get the hell over here!" Instead it was, "Okay, let's roll 'em. Extras, I need you to pick up the pace. Let's make this a good one. Now Julia, look towards Cameron and go . . ."

Holy cow, I had just found myself smack-dab in the middle of a big-time Hollywood movie set and was now an aspiring extra. As I strutted passed the cameras like I had been there before, I glanced nonchalantly to the left and noticed that the two fairly attractive divas that I was "working" with were Julia Roberts and Cameron Diaz. Trying not to blow my cover, I had plans of just taking my twenty seconds of fame and getting the hell out of there as soon as the director yelled out, "Cut!" but it wasn't that easy. I was trapped by my fellow "stars," and my escape route was blocked by movie equipment. What do I do?

As I looked up towards the "herd of cows" that the officer said I was supposed to be following, I noticed that hundreds of them were comfortably watching all the fun I was having from behind the lines. At that point I had another decision to make. Should I go back to where I was supposed to be…or take a stupid little risk and see what happens? Well, I took the risk and did what the director told me to do. "Okay, extras, I need you back in your spots." But as I walked back to my "spot," I realized that I didn't have one! I would have to steal someone else's "spot." As I got to one that looked like it would work, a little bearded man, wearing a yellow Hawaiian shirt approached with an unconfident, squeaky, and bird-like voice and said, "Excuse me sir…sir…um…it appears you're in my spot."

Oh no, I'm caught. What should I do? Should I run for the lines…get back with the cows? Luckily, I was saved when the director yelled out, "Okay extras, I need you to move on four, three, two, one…roll the camera…good, Julia…now begin walking, Cameron…" The director saved me, and I was having a blast outside these lines. After four more takes my Hollywood career was over, and I returned home. While the cows that stayed between the lines returned to their homes and their own leather couches, they no doubt told someone they loved what they had seen at O'Hare that day. By taking a risk, by being a little stupid, I was able to tell my wife what I did that day.

So what's the point? Perhaps Austrian-born, American management consultant Peter Drucker said it best:

> People who don't take risks generally make about two big mistakes a year. People who do take risks generally make about two big mistakes a year.

If you call on larger companies or corporations, where many of the decisions are made "where you ain't been"…*go there!* Quit being a wimp. The basements of your finest prospects are full of "risk averse" salespeople swarming around like a bunch of red ants, afraid of "making waves" or doing something that might get them in trouble. Don't sweat it! Find that "C" Suite, figure out a way to accidentally "bump" into a CEO. Whatever! I have two words for you, "who cares?" So much freedom comes with those words. Let yourself go a bit. That sick little pit you get in your stomach that comes from getting out of your comfort zone is called an adrenaline rush. I'm not asking you to jump out of an airplane, I just want you to "stray outside the lines" a bit.

I never went to see the movie *My Best Friend's Wedding,* but six months after it was released, a business associate and I were having dinner. Being a little "stupid" himself, he left the dinner table and was gone for at least fifteen minutes. When he returned, he was holding a portable television/VCR combo and that familiar Blockbuster video case. He popped in the tape, pressed fast forward for a few seconds, then pressed pause. I felt pretty "stupid" as waiters gathered around to see the screen shot that showed only the heads of Julia, Cameron, and me. While I may never be famous, I will always have the recorded memory of the day I decided to be a bit stupid.

(To view Julia, Cameron, and the short Irish guy in action, go to www.preciseselling.com/stupid.wmv)

Stupid Wrap-Up

- Admit who you are—a stupid salesperson.
- Stand out from other reps.
- Identify your stupidity tolerance.
- Keep looking for ways to increase that tolerance.
- Identify a day to be stupid to make it a habit.

This stupidly PRECISE posture can build a foundation that brings the walls down and helps build long-term relationships. The next chapter will discuss the importance of product, industry, and competitive knowledge. While being stupid makes sense in building relationships, it doesn't make sense as it relates to PIC Knowledge.

Be stupid in posture while being smart in PIC knowledge.

Chapter Eight
P #2—PIC Knowledge:
Why Knowing a Ton and Sharing a Little Is Better Than Knowing a Little and Sharing a Ton

> "Knowledge is power...knowledge is safety...knowledge is happiness."
> —Thomas Jefferson (1743–1826)

Already an estimated two-thirds of U.S. employees work in the services sector, and knowledge is becoming our most important "product." In sales, the first product your customer must "buy" is your knowledge of that product. You can have the greatest product or service in the world, but your product or service is only as good as the knowledge you have and the way you use it during a sales call.

> Besides product knowledge, top salespeople also need a healthy dose of industry and competition knowledge to be successful.

This PIC knowledge is one of the three Ps in the PRECISE Selling Formula of Top Performers.

When I say PIC knowledge, I am talking about PIC-ing apart your competition. It is one area that sales reps have complete control over, and yet average salespeople too often use excuses to justify why it is impossible to know everything. Many believe that they can get by with just enough to get by, but that is all they will do unless their knowledge is high-level. PRECISE Sales Reps don't just get by, they *blow by* the competition. Knowing more than the next rep allows this to happen.

Learning Starts with "Wanting"

When I was not cleaning colonoscopes, I was demonstrating the latest in ear, nose, and throat technology. One of our most popular products at the time was the RL-150, high-octane, supercharged rhinolaryngoscope. This was a smaller, flexible scope that looked like black spaghetti and was inserted into the nose and driven delicately through the nasal passages until it would hang just over the vocal cords. I found this product rather exciting but could find no one that would physically allow me to try this out on them.

It was a sunny spring day in South Bend, Indiana, and I was about to do my first demonstration on this new product. As I sat in the car, I was feeling a bit uneasy. How on earth was I going to speak knowledgeably about something I have never seen performed on a patient? It was at that moment that I decided to become that patient. It was also at that moment that I decided to become "doctor." I adjusted the seat in my sporty minivan so I could get a good view of my nose in the rearview mirror. I pulled the scope out of the box, looked through the eyepiece, and in it went.

Imagine taking a piece of slightly cooked spaghetti with an eyepiece at one end, putting it up to your eye, and then sticking the other end in your nose. Then imagine pushing that spaghetti until your eyes watered so much that you could no longer see anything. I felt like I was starring in the 1990s version of MTV's reality show *Jackass*. It was pure torture, but as a young, ambitious sales rep, it was a rite of passage. After scraping the inner walls of my nose five or six times with little progress, I decided to retreat. Although I knew no more about that product and procedure than when I started, I felt like I had just completed the Tour de France. I could now empathize better with those poor patients who would be on the receiving end of my torture device. This perspective would have to help me, right?

After returning to my home that night in Chicago, I pulled the scope out of the car again, and this time found a larger mirror to stand in front of. I turned the scope on and in I went; only this time, I was successful with a lot fewer tears. Let me tell you, I was excited when I was able to see those "V" shape vocal cords talking back at me. I was now ready to talk with enthusiasm about all the benefits that my scope would provide

to both patient and doctor. Because, damn it, I had been on both ends—
and at the same time.

While I don't believe that physical abuse is necessary to become skill-
ful in the product knowledge category, I do believe that it is important to
do more than your competition. To understand how, why, when, and where
your customers will use your product, do what other sales reps won't.

> Learning is wanting and the more you want, the more you will learn.

How Much PIC Knowledge Do You Need?

You need as much knowledge as you can obtain, but use only what your
customer can retain.

Too Little PIC Knowledge

There is nothing more frustrating as a sales rep than to have your sales presentation speeding along like an Indy car, only to have a customer throw out
question that you can't answer. It's like hitting a speed bump at a hundred
miles an hour. While this may be understandable for a newer product or
service that you are still familiarizing yourself with, it is not acceptable for
those that you have been talking about for several days or weeks.

"That's a great question," is a comment often used by the average rep
and is usually followed by, "Let me get back to you." Well, two days later
when the average rep finally has the answers and tries to "get back with"
the prospect, much of the selling momentum is long gone.

"I'm not here right now, but I will get back to you," never sounds good
when it is coming from a customer on voice mail. It's even worse when
those words are from a prospect that was standing directly in front of you
and hanging on your every word only forty-eight hours earlier.

Think of how you feel when you are on the other end of such an
exchange. You are looking for answers that will help you make an educated decision and are unable to because the sales rep did not do her home-
work. Compassion can only be shown when that sales rep looks you in the
eye, pulls out that pen and notepad, and writes down exactly what your
question is and exactly when you can expect an answer.

> "He knows so little and knows it so fluently."
>
> —Ellen Glasgow

Sometimes we screw up. Sometimes, as fate has it, we find ourselves in a customer discussion before we have had enough time to become the experts we need to be. If this occurs, do not say "so little, so fluently." Customers today are much more finicky and educated than ever before, and if we are not careful, we will sound exactly like what they expect: bullshit artists. We must tell them what we know and only if it applies to the question that was asked. We will fool nobody if we simply try to shift gears and start discussing that part of the product or service that we do feel comfortable with.

How Much PIC Knowledge Is Too Much?

> "He not only overflowed with learning, but also stood in the slop."
>
> —Sydney Smith

While it is not necessarily a bad thing to overflow with learning, it is important that you are not left standing in the slop. It is even more important that you don't spew that slop all over your customers.

Constantly nurture your product knowledge. What you know after your first sales call should not be the same as what you know after your tenth. The downside to all of this product knowledge is knowing how and when to use it. Just because you are smarter than ever, you need not feel the impulse to impress the customer with just how intelligent you are. I have seen many good salespeople become less effective the "smarter" they got. Watching them spew the slop they stood in was like watching a B-52 drop a load of cluster bombs when a precision-guided weapon would have been more effective. The key to product knowledge is to have as much as you can, never stop learning, but only use what is necessary, depending on the selling situation. Being PRECISE means having an arsenal full of weapons, even when only one is needed to complete the mission.

When Can I Learn?

While it is important to become a student of your product or service, it is not acceptable to take selling hours to do it. Which means that you should not get back from your national sales meeting where you learned about the newest widget and decide that you will not try to sell it until you feel completely confident. Your goal should not be to become the expert in the business within the first two weeks. Your goal should be to make sure that you push yourself to constantly grow and to never plateau. Never stop asking questions. While sitting in your office studying and reading may make you smarter, the best learning lies in the field, out among your customers.

Wait...and Learn

As a salesperson, you should be almost as good at waiting to see customers as you are at selling to customers. Unless you believe you know everything you need to about your product or service, you should rarely find yourself just sitting and sighing. Being parked in the lobby or lounge waiting for your prospect to open the gates to Oz doesn't have to be a bad thing. Waiting time is learning time, and it should be valued as much as selling time. So pull out a brochure or sheet of literature on that new solution of yours that you don't quite feel comfortable with yet. Grab that industry magazine that talks about how great your competitor is. Review the previous notes that you made regarding the customer you are about to visit. Whatever you do, *don't* pick up that issue of *InStyle* or *Sports Illustrated* that's sitting on the lounge table in front of you.

It will be these crucial waiting and learning moments that will separate you from your competitor when your customer is asking the tough question. While your competitor is saying, "I will follow up on that information." You will be saying, "I will follow up on that order."

Where are good places to learn?

There are four good places to learn:

1. Top producers in your company
2. Current customers
3. Internet
4. Competition

Top Producers

Champion sales reps in your organizations can be like encyclopedias. Whether you are a rookie or an experienced rep, there is much information that you can gain from the seasoned mind. Make it a habit to get on the phone, buy lunch, or meet for a drink. Do whatever you have to do to tap into the minds of your company or industry champions. The best way to ensure that you do this is to get out your Day-Timer or PDA, grab your phone list, and make time to do it. Have at least two visits or two phone calls each month with a company or industry champ.

Current Customers

What the marketing gurus in your company are telling you about a product or service is, no doubt, information that you need. However, those PowerPoint slides they put up on the big screen will not be nearly as valuable as the words from current users of your products. Most average sales reps, freshly back from product training, have a tendency to fill every moment of their first sales calls with needless chatter. PRECISE sales reps, on the other hand, spend most of their early time asking, listening, and learning from current users of similar products.

PRECISE sales reps also are not afraid to play a little dumb. They are experts at asking customers what they think about their products' abilities as if they are skeptical themselves. So while you are visiting with current customers, convey to them that you are there to get their professional opinion. Then watch them spill the goods. As they spill the goods, you get smarter. And if you are lucky, you may even get the order.

The Internet

The Internet is a great source for competitive information. Competitors are all too willing to share with you nearly everything you need to know about the features and benefits of their products.

In fact, two years ago, a new company had entered one of our most competitive cardiopulmonary markets by developing a computer-based EKG (which tests the heart) and a spirometer (which tests lung function). This device intrigued our entire sales force, and we did everything we could to find out any details. I felt like the CIA monitoring the "chatter." But despite my efforts, I could not get the information I needed to compete effectively against it.

Then it hit me: perhaps they have left some clues on their website. Well, not only did they leave clues, I found the goods. Not only was there information, there was a demo version of the entire program available for download. Not only did I now know about the product, I was able to use it right on my laptop. Four hours later, I knew everything I needed to know to effectively compete against it. I knew all the benefits and weaknesses and was now fully prepared for any question that would be thrown at me.

The Internet is also a great tool to keep you updated on industry information and trends. Nearly every industry has one or two trade publications serving it, and those publications usually have websites. Schedule at least thirty minutes of non–selling time a week to find out what is happening in your industry, and you will gain more credibility as you speak to your peers, customers, and leaders within your company. Some of these publications will even send free daily emails with the latest industry scoop. They are usually quick and to the point and the five minutes a day you dedicate to browsing through the info will separate you from the competition.

The Competition

There is nothing more refreshing to the ear than to hear important information rolling off the tongue of one of your loudmouth competitor's lips. Arrogance can be wonderful, as long as it is not you who are arrogant. Cocky salespeople have a wonderful inability to keep their mouths shut. As a competitor, you should learn to take advantage of it. You should never find yourself acting as if you are standing in the schoolyard fighting over whose daddy can beat up the other. Let the competition tell you how strong her daddy is, what makes him so powerful, and then agree with her that she has one strong daddy. While that competitor is feeding her ego, you are feeding your mind with valuable information that will be used against her later in the court of sales.

For centuries, armies primarily used battle lines to attack and defend. We all have seen movies or documentaries showing these soldiers lined up, prepared to just stand or march to their death. It amazes me every time I watch, as the soldiers just walk slowly ahead, the ones in front getting shot, leaving the next line of soldiers to fill their place. I am all for dignity and honor, but this type of fighting was just plain nuts. As rifle power became more deadly and more accurate, military leaders realized there were more effective ways to defeat the enemy, and it rarely included walking slowly out in the open, straight at the arsenal of the enemy. In fact, flank attacks, or trying to go behind or to the side of the enemy, proved more successful.

In sales, we sometimes need to flank our competition. And to flank, we need to sometimes be a bit creative. In 1994, I had a demonstration scheduled with a very important customer. This customer was going to be spending a large sum of money with either my company or a competitor. This was truly a head-to-head battle, as both companies were given the opportunity on the same day to present their solution to a group of five physicians and financial managers. I stewed over this call because I felt like I did not know enough about the competition. I was sure this would kill me. This was a couple of years before the Internet had become a common research tool, and I had expended all other research resources.

Well, it was time for the flanking move. I picked up the phone, dialed the competitor's customer service department, and fired away. And let me tell you, they were as friendly as they were helpful. I asked almost every question that I thought my VIP customer would ask and got every answer I was looking for. I even found some things out about my company and product that I didn't even know existed! In fact, they didn't exist, but it was nice to know that these untruths would probably come up with the customer. While some may find this tactic a bit unfair, I see it as a tactic of the sales battle. And that was one battle, that in the end, I won.

The Wright brothers once said, "It is possible to fly without motors, but not without knowledge and skill."

There are two simple parts to Orville and Wilber's formula.

1. Know your stuff

2. Be skilled in using that knowledge

So do your best to know more than anybody in your company and industry. Set the bar high and plan a little time each week to do nothing but research. This means no voice mail, no email, and no catching up on the latest episode of *The View*. And when you effectively combine that continually growing knowledge with the superior selling skills that I am about to teach you, you will be well on your way to becoming your company's top sales performer…quickly.

Chapter Nine
PRECISE Actions:
The Seven Commission-Building Actions That You Will Easily Remember and Repeat on Every Sales Call

W e have so far discussed two of the three Ps of the PRECISE Selling Formula of Top Performers. We focused on the importance of PRECISE Posture in getting prospects to open up and better relate to you. We also discussed the value of obtaining as much PIC Knowledge as possible, while sharing only what your customers can retain.

It is now time to discuss our third P. This is the real "meat" of PRECISE Selling. The following chapters tell you exactly what to do and say when it is "game time." So let the games begin.

The Seven Actions That Will Make You Your Company's Top Performer in 20 Days or Less Are:

1. Prepare
2. Respect and Trust
3. Engage with Questions and Curiosity
4. Convey Solution
5. Indecision—Overcome Yours and Theirs
6. Secure and Advance
7. Explore

PRECISE is the acronym for the seven Actions that I will teach you in the following chapters. While many sales reps do not like to be cornered into any sales process, I will assure you that I will not take away your humanity and turn you into a Cyborg or some mindless character from the movie *The Matrix*. When you carry product knowledge, your posture, and deliver your awesome package in an *exact* and *sharply defined* way, you will be unstoppable. I will make everything out of your mouth mean something when in front of the customer. The seven PRECISE Actions will put power into every syllable that rolls off your tongue and help you achieve results that will benefit you and your customers. By being PRECISE, you will say more while saying less.

What's so special about the seven PRECISE Actions? *They work!* They are not a bunch of sales guru fluff. A research firm studying over ten thousand sales specimens under interrogation lights did not design these. A real-life salesperson developed them. They are the result of years of trial and error, and I have watched them change my sales life and the lives of so many others. We'll go into detail on each step in the coming chapters, but first there are some important points to understand.

Why Is a Process Necessary in Sales?

> "He had no more sense of direction than a bunch of firecrackers."
> —Rob Wagner

Every Fourth of July my wife and I take the kids to Missouri, where fireworks are legal. This is a trip my wife dreads but one I find exhilarating. Now, I don't like to mess with the stuff that can blow the moles off my body. I only like to dabble with the few little harmless ones that, even if they blew up in my hand, wouldn't do more than make me cry like a four-year-old.

If you too like to dabble in a bit of the pyro, you know that adrenaline-pumping anticipation that you get after you light that baby up. The truth is, you have no clue what is coming. You just pull the goodie out of its package, light the wick, and run like hell. Sometimes that little firecracker goes off just like the package said it would. Other times the tiny explosive just fizzles out…at least long enough for you to go up, check out what's wrong, and then have it blow up in your face.

Well, average and below-average salespeople often act like firecrackers. They get in front of a customer, light the wick, and hope for the best.

Sometimes what comes out of their mouths is pure beauty. But most times, they just have no clue what is going to happen.

If you master the techniques that I am about to share with you, you will not be as inconsistent as a firecracker. Hell, no! You will have found a process that allows you to still be you. You will have found a series of actions that create great selling habits that are measurable, repeatable, and sustainable.

To Keep Improving, Learn from Every Sales Call

"Learn all your life. Learn from your failures, from your successes. Life is an error-making and error-correcting process."
—John W. Gardner (1912–2002), former U.S. Secretary of Health, Education, and Welfare, in his commencement remarks at Stanford University

Progress can occur every time you make a sales call, regardless of how well you perform. The main difference between the average sales Joe and the PRECISE sales rep is his ability to improve every time he either hangs up that phone or starts the car's ignition. During every customer meeting, it is important that you take the good actions and behaviors that you did and internalize them, so you increase your chances that you will do it again next sales call. At the same time, it is nearly impossible to do everything correctly in a sales call. Thus, there is always something that you can improve on.

Why is it that most sales reps stop improving at some point in their sales career? It's because they have stopped learning. Why have they stopped learning? Because they have stopped looking for ways to learn, or are looking in the wrong place. Make learning a habit.

Create Good Habits

I am here always.
I can make or break you.
I can motivate you to greatness or stifle your growth.
I am difficult to create and even harder to break.
I work on impulse and need little direction.
I have a good memory and am repeatable.
I am the most valued asset of the professional.
I am the greatest burden of the weak.
Use me as a weapon against mediocrity.
Use me as your map on the road to excellence.
With me, you will own the competition.
I am PRECISE.
What am I?
A habit.

There is an old saying, "Practice makes perfect." There is another saying, "Perfect practice makes perfect." Both of the sayings make perfect sense in the sales world. Truth is, most salespeople practice nothing and believe there is nothing a salesperson can, in fact, practice. They believe that you were either born to be in sales or you were not. They think, "How can you practice relationship and people skills? These things just come naturally." While relationship skills are essential to being PRECISE, it is the true professional who finds a repeatable, measurable, and sustainable habit and action plan when serving customers.

It is possible to use the same fundamental tactics on different customers, while treating each one individually. The seven actions of PRECISE Selling are sound fundamental tactics that when practiced, internalized, and put to work in front of a customer, will produce happier customers and more confident sales representatives. These fundamentals, however, are only effective if they become habit. Without them becoming a habit, they, like so many other sales tactics, are difficult to sustain.

So when you finish reading this book, you will have choices to make. You might choose to adapt the selling system that was laid out in its pages.

You might choose to use only some of the actions that you learned. You might close the cover, wishing you never wasted your time flipping through the pages. Or you might just head back to the bookstore in search of some other book that you think will help put more money in your pocket.

Whatever you do, find *something* that you can turn into a habit or selling process. If you study, internalize, remember, try, hone, and perfect the seven PRECISE Actions outlined in this book, you will sell more than you ever dreamed possible. And in the end, your existing customers will appreciate you more than ever, and your future clients will come to understand that your supreme goal is to find and provide only those products and services that will improve their lives. You will deliver high-powered, PRECISE solutions while using fewer words than ever before.

Find Something That Works, and Then Repeat It

Tiger Woods began playing golf at the age of one. His father, Earl Woods, was a skilled teacher and a true believer of the power of habit. While his goal was perhaps not to create the greatest golf professional that ever lived, that's exactly what he did. Earl focused in on two specific areas. First, he made sure that Tiger always respected and trusted him. Tiger never doubted his father's intent and therefore he was "coachable." While some might compare Earl's coaching style to that of Bobby Knight, it was this disciplined and repeatable approach to golf and life that has made Tiger a success.

Earl Woods is a believer in habit and instilled several repeatable, measurable, and sustainable actions into Tiger's golf game. When Tiger was putting, Earl made sure that Tiger looked at the putt from every angle while on the putting surface. While on the tee box, Earl made sure that Tiger teed up the ball, walked behind it, mentally pictured the shot, and then and only then could he address the ball. These are just two examples of some important repeatable actions that Tiger needed to take before he ever struck the golf ball.

Could Tiger Woods sink a three-foot putt between his legs or behind his back? Can he bounce a ball off his 7-iron into the air and pound it 170 yards? The answer to both of these questions is yes. So why doesn't Tiger Woods occasionally try this while he is on the golf course during a professional event? The answer is simple. He doesn't do it because if he did, it would decrease his odds of being successful.

Salespeople try three-foot putts between their legs and behind their backs all the time. When their customers either walk in the door or pick up the phone, they have no repeatable "putting" technique or method to rely on. In sales, you need to do as Earl Woods taught Tiger. To be a professional and to be the best in your sales profession, you need to putt the three-footers the same way each time. You need to address your customers in a repeatable way, just as Tiger Woods addresses his golf ball in a repeatable way. When actions are repeatable, they become easy. When actions are easy for you, you gain confidence. With confidence, you stay in control in front of your customers. With this control, it is easier to get to the point of what your customer is looking for, and then design a focused presentation. By doing this, you will say only what your customer wants to hear—no more, no less.

Performance Is Measurable

It is easy for you as a sales representative to measure your success. Either you are achieving your sales objectives or you are not. But what about the specific actions that were performed in that sales call? Shouldn't they be measured? Can they be measured? Yes, they can. The PRECISE Actions help you identify what selling activity needs to go, and what selling actions need to stay. By identifying what actions you need to perform in a sales call, and by then reviewing if you performed them, you are able to measure how well you did, and what specific areas you need to improve on.

After a sales call, it is easy to review your performance and say you did four of them well, but need to improve on three specific areas. In your next call, you want to repeat the four good actions, and try to improve on at least one that you came up short on. Hard sales numbers are easy for a sales rep to get her hands around, but measuring the "How did you do it?" can sometimes be difficult. It doesn't have to be. By constantly keeping the seven PRECISE Actions in front of you throughout your selling day, you can measure the specific steps that either made or broke you during your last sales call.

Measure Your Performance; Then Measure the Size of Your Commission Check

Many measurable actions occur in a football game. A player or coach can look back over a four-quarter game and with a fair amount of certainty put his finger on what specific plays contributed to the success or the failure of the overall outcome of the game.

It is not so simple for the average sales representative. Things just are not that black and white. What is so disheartening to so many sales reps is that they can't put their finger on what is either making them successful or unsuccessful. In my sales seminars, I often ask the top sales reps in the group what makes them so good. The responses that I usually get have little "meat." In other words, there is little that anyone in the training room can get their hands on, practice, master, and take to their customers on Monday morning. Frankly, most of these top gun sales reps have no idea what makes them successful.

When I ask those that are not meeting their sales numbers what they think it is that is keeping them back, their response is equally ambiguous. Most often, these salespeople have no clue about what separates them from those at the top of the pack. Without a strategy and some specific tactics to help achieve specific objectives, you will have nothing to measure. If you have nothing to measure, it is impossible to improve. Keep measuring not only your sales numbers, but also those specific actions that create those numbers.

Look at your job as a football season. Split the year into four quarters. Develop a specific game plan. Practice the specific PRECISE Actions and fundamentals that I will teach you in this book. Execute them. Review the "game film" each Monday morning, and adjust your strategy accordingly. If you follow these steps, you will be able to confidently answer the questions, "What is making me so successful?" and "Where do I need to improve?"

No Sustain, No Gain...in Your Pay!

Companies all over the world spend millions of dollars yearly on sales training. There is the new "flavor of the month" selling system or technique that is going to provide the magic bullet in helping a company achieve its sales objectives. These companies take their sales forces out of the field, fly them in from all over the country, put them up in fancy hotels, wine them, dine them, chain them to their seats in a classroom, and tell them that what they will learn is going to transform their lives. Unfortunately, what most of the high-priced, so-called sales gurus deliver is nothing more than a dose of sales Viagra. They get salespeople all pumped up, but more often than not, the performance-enhancing techniques that they deliver are often gone long before the sun comes up.

As a salesperson myself, I am constantly looking for the hard-core, specific tools that will help me sell more stuff. If you are training me and all you have is a bunch of feel-good, transcendental, toe-touching, politically correct "communications" principles, "forget about it!" Or if you send me away with some new calisthenics to perform in the shower that will help me better empathize with a customer, I won't buy it. In short, my thoughts are, "Save the bullshit and tell me exactly what *you did* that made you blow the doors off your sales numbers when you were a sales rep." If you are teaching me something that you have never used yourself, and have no proof of the direct impact these skills had on your success, no thank you! If it sounds like I am mocking the world of sales training, it is because I am.

If you are looking for sales actions that are sustainable, that will improve your sales performance for more than one night, I encourage you to internalize the PRECISE Actions outlined in this book. If you commit to the seven PRECISE Actions, practice them, and are willing to go through the pain that comes with change, you will feel more confident in front of customers than ever before. It will lead to fatter commission checks that will pump you up. And in the end, that is what PRECISE Selling is all about.

How Do I Know This Works?

"I think we're going to have to let him go," were the words that I heard from one rep's sales manager in 1997. The person that they were talking about was one of the nicest people I have ever met. Tim was a dedicated worker, genuinely cared about his customers, and had a great attitude. What he lacked at the time was "street savvy" and an ability to think on his feet. What I mean in English is that his communication skills were lacking. The second a customer threw him an objection or asked him a question that he could not answer, he froze up as if he were having some weird, total-body muscle spasm.

At the time, I was performing two roles within my company. I was an Equipment Specialist, which was someone who focused solely on closing high-dollar sales opportunities. And when I was not doing this, I spent time traveling with sales reps, watching their performance in front of customers, and then offering support in specific areas where we agreed they needed improvement.

After hearing that Tim was on the brink of being fired, I asked his manager to give me a shot at helping him. I felt the seven PRECISE Actions were exactly what he needed. I had a great relationship with Tim at the time and would openly and affectionately call him Forrest Gump. I called him this because he had the attitude of Forrest Gump. He would do anything and everything that was asked of him and his intentions were always selfless. Up to that point, our company had not done a good enough job helping him internalize the selling skills that he had been taught. Once he realized that his job was on the line, he was ready to try anything.

After spending several days riding with him in his sales territory and drilling into his head the seven actions that I will share with you, this rep committed to make PRECISE Selling his career saver. He said that he would dedicate the next 20 days to internalizing and practicing the PRECISE Actions. If it didn't work, he didn't know what he would do.

When I traveled with him on that first day, he was dead last in sales in our company. After 20 days of practicing and using the seven PRECISE Actions, something had noticeably changed as he began slowly moving up the sales ranking list. Only six months later, this rep who was so close to being fired was now no longer last in the company in sales, but was now first.

It was a classic "worst-to-first story." What was even more impressive was the way Tim now carried himself in front of his customers. He was one of the most PRECISE sales reps that I have seen to date. Every word out of Tim's mouth advanced the sale, and as a result, his customers loved him. He wasted nobody's time and provided only those solutions that made sense to the people he served.

For those who had known the old Tim, and then got the chance to see the new PRECISE Tim, it was nothing short of freaky. He was a different salesperson. His confidence, his attitude, and his posture were purely pro-fessional, and the actions that he used to get him to that higher level were repeatable, measurable, and sustainable. Although I helped Tim with the PRECISE fundamentals that would become the foundation of his sales presentations, it was Tim who made the commitment to making PRECISE

Selling a habit.

About a year later, I got a call from Tim on my cell phone. He told me that he would be leaving our company and that he found a higher-paying sales position with another prominent medical company. As he was telling me about his new position, his voice began to crack. He began thanking me for giving him the tools that helped make him more confident, helped keep his job, and helped him become a top rep in the company.

Although I hated to hear that Tim would be leaving, that was one of the greatest days in my professional career. While I might have played a small part in Tim's improvement, I have no doubt that it was his commitment to the PRECISE Formula that caused his success. Tim convinced me that anybody could use this formula to dominate and become a top performer. He also convinced me that if I want to keep my reps working for me, I better be careful not to make too many of them PRECISE. They will end up leaving for a higher-paying job!

The Greatest Product

I have sold many different products in my years as a sales professional, and most of them I was proud to represent. Of all the products I have sold, PRECISE Selling is the greatest. While the devices that I represented provided real value to my customers, none have done what this product, PRECISE Selling, has done for the customers and salespeople that I have served. Doctors, nurses, hospitals, and clinics can quickly forget the value of a piece of medical instrumentation. But the salespeople that "buy into" the product within these pages will see and feel a difference in the way they perform for an entire career. If you want to do a better job representing your product or service, then give PRECISE Selling a chance to do what it has done for so many salespeople. Give yourself a chance for more confidence, more sales, and lots more fun.

Chapter Ten
PRECISE Action #1: Prepare Like Vince Lombardi...You Animal!

Main Entry: prepare

Function: verb

1: the action or process of making something ready for use or service or of getting ready for some occasion, test, or duty.

Test or duty? When you are in front of an important customer, do you ever feel as if you are taking a test? It can sometimes feel like an oral exam from your days in high school or college. Well, we can all remember a time or two (in my case, perhaps a few more) when we walked into that final exam not feeling like we put in the study time necessary to perform well. Can you remember that sick, helpless feeling that you had when you looked at the first three questions on that sheet of paper, only to have your face and ears heat up like a rotisserie oven? You swore to yourself that you would never again put yourself in that position. And you swore even louder when your score came back three days later. If you had only taken the time to go to the library to prepare!

Well, here we are as sales professionals years later, and the stakes are even higher. That same sick feeling is waiting for us every time we walk through the doors of our customers when we neglect the first step of the PRECISE Actions.

"Victory is what happens when preparation meets opportunity."
—Vince Lombardi (1913–1970), professional football coach

Action #1

Preparation is the first phase of any sale, the most controllable phase, and yet the most neglected. During a sales call a lot can happen. The customer will try to pull you a dozen different directions. But if you have put enough quality time into preparing for the sales call, you will find that you will have more control over yourself, your mouth, and your customer.

Preparation for the salesperson is like boot camp for a marine. It can take a long time, be tiresome and painful, and frankly just isn't very fun. But it is only when the marine finds himself in the middle of the battle that he appreciates the hours he spent preparing. While your lack of preparation as a salesperson might not cost you your life, as is the case with the marine, it can cost you a sale or two. And sometimes it can cost you your job. Never let your lack of preparation be the reason you fail. It is too easy to control, and it makes sales a lot more fun when enough time is dedicated to it.

Sell Yourself

Sell yourself before you sell your customer. To convey a message that will excite your customers and make them want to do business with you and your company, you must believe in what you are selling. The first person that needs to "be sold" on any product or service needs to be the person that is selling. As you think about your product or service, you need to first present that product to the most discriminating of all customers—you.

Now this might seem a bit strange, but who cares? Go ahead, go over to the mirror and sell yourself something. Okay, so that might seem a bit extreme. Maybe you don't need to talk out loud, but it wouldn't kill you to mentally perform at least three sales calls in your mind before you make your first one on any new product or service. And when you do this, don't go easy on yourself. Ask hard questions that demand comprehensive and convincing answers. As you do this, you'll find that you just might not be satisfied with the answers you are coming up with.

This dissatisfaction will force you to hone your presentation, reduce the needless chatter that so many sales reps love to spew, and in the end will build the foundation of what will become a PRECISE presentation. It is only after you sell yourself that you will be able to PRECISE-ly represent the product or service that will eventually put money in your pocket.

Set Objectives Before Sales Calls

Sales calls, whether on the phone or in person, should rarely be made without a written objective. This written objective could be as simple as a few words in your planner or as comprehensive as a few bullet points stored in a presentation binder.

In my years as a sales trainer, I have had the opportunity to witness hundreds of sales calls. While nearly every one of them had a purpose, not every one of them had an objective. By this I mean that all reps have their reasons for pulling up to the front door of a customer or picking up that phone, be it a new prospect or existing customer. But many reps do not define what that objective is.

I will never forget a sales call I made early in my career with thirty-year sales veteran turned Welch Allyn VP of Sales, John Moran. John was and still is one of the most respected leaders in the medical industry and is an expert at relationship selling. Despite his "Godfather" status, this guy is not afraid to jump in the passenger seat and share some wisdom with reps of all experience levels. He is also not afraid to "booby trap" your car or briefcase if you are not careful (I once found a half-eaten banana in my attaché case two days after he left). And John is PRECISE. He says only what is necessary to help his reps and no more. He is not a sales leader who loves to hear himself speak. He understands that salespeople are his customers and if he is to influence them, less is often more, just as in selling. He is PRECISE because he makes every word and every piece of advice mean something.

When John traveled with you, it was an honor and an experience you did not want to screw up. On one sales day, we were calling on an important distribution customer with whom I had a very good relationship. I told the customer that I would be in the area around two o'clock with the bigwig and that I wanted to stop by to visit with him. Two o'clock rolled around, we stopped by for about thirty minutes and then left. I felt like a million bucks and thought for sure "The Godfather" would feel the same way. After asking for his feedback on how the call went, I thought I would I feel like Barry Bonds being thrown a hanging curveball. I was just waiting for his praise so I could start my march around the bases.

Well, the batting lesson had just begun. When John asked me "What was the objective of the call?" I froze up like I was the first man living on the planet Pluto. After bumbling for a few seconds, I told him that I just wanted to stop by to see how our customer was doing.

He said, "What was your objective in seeing how he was doing?"

I said, "To make sure he still liked our company and what we were doing."

"What does that mean? What was your objective in seeing if he still liked our company and what we were doing?" John responded.

This little exercise was driving me nutty, but the man in the passenger seat was my boss's boss's boss, so I had better play the game.

I said, "By liking us, it is easier for me to get him to commit to running a sixty-day promotion on our scopes."

John said, "So why wasn't our objective to get him to commit to a sixty-day promotion on our scopes?"

I said, "Because I didn't think of it."

He said, "You just did."

Wow! This guy just used questioning techniques masterfully to lead me to a more specific objective.

As I looked back on that sales call with John, I realized I had accomplished little. I made the mistake so many sales reps make. Without a well thought out and written objective, I was set up for failure and just going through the motions.

> Never make a sales call without a clear and measurable objective that results in customer action.

Vince Lombardi used to say, "Winning is fun and losing is not." When a football game is over, one team wins and the other loses. There is nothing confusing about it. In sales, it is not so black and white. Assessing your success or failure depends on the objective you set for your sales call. The reason many salespeople are in their profession is because they love the feeling they get when they succeed. There is no better feeling than walking out of the call knowing that you did everything right and, in the end, have a customer and a commission check to show for it.

Success, however, can come even without a written order. In today's complex selling environments, it is often difficult to get to all decision-makers and receive an order after only one or two sales calls. In some selling situations it could be a five-, eight-, or ten-call process. If you have a clear objective, and that objective advances the sale and takes you closer to payday each time, then you met your objective. Feel free to give that fist of yours a little pump.

Know the Game Conditions

One reason salespeople fail is that they don't know enough about their customers. Salespeople need to know as much about the prospect as they do about their own product or service. Before making that first call on a prospect try to find out:

- What keeps the prospect up at night? What are the biggest challenges he or she faces every day?
- What does that prospect value? What benefits are most important?
- How are decisions made on products or services like yours?
- Is there an expressed need for your product or service?
- Has he or she looked at any competitor's product or service?

Know the Opponent

"Beat your opponent where he is strongest, and you demoralize him."
—Vince Lombardi (1913–1970), professional football coach

If you are to beat your opponent where he is strongest, you need to know your opponent. Great football coaches like Vince Lombardi would never enter a game not knowing the strengths and weaknesses of the competition. It is the preparation that occurs long before game time that will give you the confidence you will need if a discussion about your competitor's product comes up. There are few things worse than a prospect knowing something about your competitor that you do not.

Check the Weather before You Put Your Pads On

Football is sometimes played in 100-degree weather, and it is sometimes played in subzero weather. When preparing for the game, these weather factors should be considered. The best research a football coach can do is to turn on the local news broadcast and check the weather.

Salespeople also need to check the weather. For instance, when calling on other companies, here are ways to do it:

Go online and look at that company's website. Their "Home" page, "About Us," "Company Information," "Founders," sections are all great resources of information. Make note of the names and titles of the key people on that website. Those names will come in handy during your sales call.

While online, look for any recent press releases or news articles that might tell you the challenges and successes the company is experiencing. They might be having their worst year in a decade. Can you imagine if the first question out of your mouth was, "How's business?" You don't want to send them into a funk because you had no clue about their situation.

Call their customer service department to fill in the blanks, but be specific in your questioning. Remember, PRECISE reps waste nobody's time.

Getting this information is not always possible before making that first call. Just do your best to ask as many questions of as many people as you can before ever walking in that door or picking up that phone. The supreme goal is to be of value to your prospect. You cannot do this if you are spending the only fifteen minutes you have with them doing nothing more than fact-finding. While I do understand that some calls are just that, fact-finding calls, it does not mean that salespeople should waste their customers' time getting information that they could have gotten long before the call.

Be Dr. Doolittle — Prepare to Talk to the Animals

Several years ago I was making a sales call with a colleague. The prospect that we were calling on was what you might call…well…a jerk. This guy had no interest in our product or service, and I believe he called is into his office just to blow off a little steam. Well, he did.

As we walked out of the office building, my buddy looked to me and said, "Man, that guy was an animal." I paused for a moment and thought about what he had said.

I responded with, "What type of animal do you think he is?"

He paused for a moment and said, "How about a *jackass*?"

We made several more sales calls that day. While it was medical office buildings that we were going into, you would have thought we were calling on the Omaha Zoo. Every time we got into the car after a call, we would identify our last customer as a specific animal. That day we had conversations with the jackass, the snake, the pussycat, the rat, the goat, the sheep, the fox, the bear, and the roach (okay, so we ran into a few insects too).

Thinking of the calls we made that day, it would have been nice to know what animal my buddy and I would be meeting with before we ever walked in the door. This preparation would have changed our mind-set and prepared us for how we should have acted and responded to the actions of the animals. With so many different personality types, it is important that we change how we look, act, and talk depending on the animal that we are presenting to. Yes, we need to become the animal that we are selling to…that is unless they are really bad animals!

Don't take too long to transform yourself from salesperson to animal. This change needs to occur almost instantaneously as the prospect either walks through that door or finishes his first sentence over the phone. Otherwise, you risk losing the ability to get your message across because the defense walls never come down. Anyway, let's talk about different prospects of the animal kingdom and what you need to do when preparing to sell to them.

The Jackass

Pronunciation: jack·ass

1: A male ass or donkey

2: A foolish or stupid person; a blockhead

Now I know that you have sold to more than a few of this type of animal before. In fact, the jackass is one of my favorites. I look forward to calling on him. Some of my funniest sales calls have resulted in the jackass doing everything he can to get me off his back. This is the one animal that I encourage you not to be like when you are in front of him. While the rule of thumb is to try to assimilate your customer, I do not encourage you to try to "out-jackass" the jackass. I encourage you to be patient with him. He has often had a tough day in the barn and looks at you as a little fly buzzing around his eyeballs. The jackass usually talks quickly, likes to get to the point, and hates the crap that he is standing in. So if you have any hope of turning the jackass into a stallion, you must speed up your speech, be PRECISE, get to the point, and not add to the crap that he is standing in. Convince him that you have a shovel and flyswatter and that you are the rep that can turn his barn into a better place.

The Snake

Pronunciation: 'snAk

1: any of numerous limbless scaled reptiles with a long tapering body and with salivary glands often modified to produce venom which is injected through grooved or tubular fangs

2: a worthless or treacherous fellow

Have you sold to any snakes? The snake, like the jackass, is an exception to the rule. While it is not in your best interest to try to be a worthless or treacherous fellow as the definition describes, it is in your best interest to talk like the snake. I have seen many snakes stare down and pounce on sales reps who were acting like pussycats. If you want the snake to respect you, look him in the eye and do not flinch. Wipe off that smile, put on your game face, and be as PRECISE as possible. The snake will never like you, but she just might respect you. That's the most you will ever get out of the snake. But once the snake respects you, she is often loyal, and always willing to bite the head off that mousy competitor that has been running around your field.

The Rat

Pronunciation: 'rat

1: any of numerous rodents (Rattus and related genera) differing from the related mice by considerably larger size and by structural details (as of the teeth) b: any of various similar rodents

2: a contemptible person: as a: one who betrays or deserts friends or associates

Don't be a rat, but make the rat trust you. The rat will give you all sorts of information about people in his workplace and about the competition. Be careful of the rat's attitude, however. They are negative and can pull you into their sewer. Don't go there. It's dark, and damp, and it's difficult to get out once you're down there. The rat has the ability to make helpless salespeople say things that they should not. Many reps believe that if they act like the rat and talk like the rat, the rat will like them. Let's get this straight. The rat likes no one, and will use anything you say to him against you. Don't trust the rat, but make the rat trust you.

The Fox

Pronunciation: 'fäks

1: any of various carnivorous mammals (especially genus Vulpes) of the dog family related to but smaller than wolves with shorter legs, more pointed muzzle, large erect ears, and long bushy tail

2: a clever crafty person

You better be sharp and clever around the fox. The fox is usually a great prospect if you are a great sales rep. The fox rarely gets tripped up and is looking for other foxes to help him find solutions to his problems. When working with the fox, you had better prepare, because he has places to go, people to see, and gets bored easily with the turtle. Once you sell to the fox, be careful to not get complacent. The clever fox is always looking for an easier, more cost-effective, and more timesaving solution. If you let the fox get out of your sight, he will run off into the woods with your competition.

The Pussycat

Pronunciation: 'pu-sⵉ-≤kat

1: a carnivorous mammal (Felis catus) long domesticated as a pet and for catching rats and mice

2: one that is weak, compliant, or amiable

Matching the pussycat is extremely important. If your tendency is to be a snake, a laughing hyena, or a circus monkey, it's time to take it down a notch. The pussycat usually talks softly, which means you need to talk softly. The pussycat gets scared easily and just hates it when the dogs play around in her office. Respect the pussycat's space and let her know that you will do nothing to hurt her. You might even bring a little catnip in for her on occasion.

The Sheep

Pronunciation: 'shEp

1: any of various ruminant mammals (genus Ovis) related to the goats but stockier and lacking a beard in the male

2: a timid defenseless creature b: a timid docile person; especially: one easily influenced or led

You need to handle that sheep a lot like the pussycat. The sheep is timid and as a result is easily frightened by the stereotypical sales rep. Be careful about the tone of your voice, and respect the sheep's personal space. One good quality about the sheep is that once he trusts you, he is easily influenced.

The Scapegoat

Pronunciation: 'gOt

1: goat: any of various hollow-horned ruminant mammals (especially of the genus Capra) related to the sheep but of lighter build and with backwardly arching horns, a short tail, and usually straight hair

2: scapegoat—one that bears the blame for others

Scapegoats exist in every company. These are the downtrodden that you see mulling the halls of your customer's facility. The scapegoat is blamed for everything that goes wrong and often has a chip on her goat shoulder. As a result, the scapegoat will often share valuable information. It is important, however, that you weed through what you hear and not buy into everything that is said. Be empathetic with the scapegoat, but don't get pulled into any office politics. Let the scapegoat know that she can trust you and try to brighten her day every now and then.

You Know What to Bring into a Sales Call...Now Bring It

Now that we have discussed how to act with these animal-like prospects, let's talk about another vital part of preparation; what to bring with you to the "hunt." I will not preach to you about the materials that you need to bring into a sales call. You have been doing your job a lot longer than I have been doing your job, which means you know how much is too much and how much is too little. I like to err on the too much side. I like to have more than enough sheets of literature should I happen to get many people excited about what I have to say. I like to have a professional-looking notepad and pen. And I like to have what I call a presentation binder. The presentation binder is any classy looking three-ring book that contains literature, brochures, competitive information, financial information, cost justification sheets, list of happy users, and my all-time favorite, testimonial letters from happy users. I will cover these in a later chapter.

PRECISE Action Review

1. Prepare
   - Specific and measurable call objective
   - Match the speech and behavior of your "animal" to bring the walls down
2. All materials ready

Chapter Eleven
PRECISE Action #2:
Respect and Trust—How to Get
Prospects to Love You,
Then Let You Do Your Job

Main Entry: 're·spect
Function: noun
1a: admiration felt or shown for someone or something that you believe
has sound, principled ideas or qualities

Hey, sales guy! That's right, I'm talking to you. You know, you with the polyester suit that would go up in flames if you lit a match. Never mind that cheesy smile so fake that you look like you were smuggled out of a wax museum. Because my name is not Dr. Phil, I will not focus on the importance of people respecting and trusting you in your daily life. I am quite confident you already know this. However, as a fellow salesperson, it is my duty to tell you (as if you had no idea already) that it is nearly impossible to sell anybody anything unless they respect and trust you. In the business world, this is a life-and-death matter. Without these two things, you might as well be lying in bed in a full-body cast. Because that is what it would be like if all the folks who had any impact on your income had no R&T for you. Customers need not look at you as their best friend, but they better know that you are true to your word.

Respect Comes from Good Ideas and Qualities

Look at the definition of respect. Sound, principled ideas are the bedrock of respect. If you have sound, principled ideas, people will often think you have good qualities. If you have good qualities, people will admire you. If they admire you, then they respect you. Think of the people that you respect the most. For many, it is a parent, a parent-like figure, a coach, an older brother or sister, a manager…whatever! These are people that you did not always agree with, yet you always admired. And it is because long after you thought they were out of their minds, you realized that they *did* have good ideas—ideas that helped you in ways that you never thought possible.

So if you are to gain the respect of your customers, you have to convince them that your ideas are sound and principled. These ideas must benefit the people whose respect you are trying to gain. Keep adding value to the people you serve and keep coming up with new ideas to make your customers' lives better.

Trust Comes from Customer Reliance

> Main Entry: 'trust
> Function: noun
> 1a: assured reliance on the character, ability, strength, or truth of someone or something

Reliance forces people to give up control. When you trust others, you hand the ball off and must live with the outcome. As a result, trust is often difficult to give, especially if by nature you are more comfortable being in control. Well, think of the customers you serve every day. Any "control freaks" there? I'll bet there are. And I'll bet the day you gained the trust of one of those freaks was like winning the lottery. Okay, maybe not the Powerball, but I am sure it felt damn good. What did you do to gain her trust?

I will tell you. You convinced her of some specific things. Ability, strength, and truth are the cornerstones of trust that you displayed. Trust is essential in business. Prospects need to know you can perform for them (ability), are not a wimp (strength), and don't bullshit them (truth). Do these things and the natural tendency of customers to distrust you as a salesperson will evaporate. The walls will come down, and then and only then will you be able to do business. If you don't first work on Action #2 (Respect and Trust) of being PRECISE, it is difficult to get through steps #3–#7.

So how do you do this?

Be a Vending Machine, Not a Slot Machine

When you put your dollar bill into that soda machine and press the button, you expect that pop (for my Midwestern friends) bottle to clang around and find its way to a place where you can grab it. Now sometimes that darn bottle gets hung up in there, and you have to fiddle with it. Despite that, you feel confident that unless the sold out button flashes red, the machine is going to spit out exactly what you ordered. This is how your customers should feel when doing business with you. Any time and effort they invest in you needs to return exactly what they expect.

In fact, if you want to be a champion sales rep, give them even more than they expect. Be a vending machine that surprises them. Imagine how happy you would have been if when you put in your dollar bill, you received not only that soda that you bought but also a free frosted mug garnished with a fruity umbrella. And what if it didn't cost you a nickel more? Now that's a surprise. That's a vending machine that most people would like to go back to. Be that vending machine with all of your customers, and continue to find ways to give them more than they expect.

Never Overstate and Underdeliver

Anticipation and disappointment are two words that should never go together. One definition of anticipation is "pleasurable expectation." Well, there is little worse than looking forward to something that doesn't happen. We can all recall times dating back to our childhood when we were psyched up for something, only to be disappointed. As a kid growing up in Connecticut, I spent many winter nights sitting on the couch watching the weather forecast on the evening news. There were special nights when I would grow uncontrollably excited as Chief Meteorologist Dr. Mel Goldstein told me that when I woke up the next morning, there would be eight to twelve inches of snow waiting for me.

There were more than a few times when that Dr. Hell (as I liked to call him) screwed it all up, got me all excited, and just flat-out blew it! I am getting emotional just thinking about how I felt when Mom told me, "Get dressed, the bus will be here shortly," as if she had no idea my heart had just been torn right out of my scrawny chest.

In sales, you must never let your customer feel this way. Never tell them that eight to twelve inches of snow is on the way, only to deliver a light dusting. They will never forget and will never trust you again. Instead, tell them that you expect three to four inches, and when you deliver that blizzard (like the Blizzard of '78...oh, baby, was that a good one), they will never forget you.

> It is much better to undersell and overdeliver THAN to oversell and underdeliver.

Smiles Work!

Want to be the most popular person at a party? Smile. I am not talking about a big, phony, cheesy smile. I am talking about an honest, warm, sincere one. Smiling has a positive effect on people. It can even make a fairly unattractive man like myself look half-good, and that takes remarkable power. Think of the last party that you went to. When was the last time you saw somebody across the room that had a big warm smile on his face and thought, "That person over there looks like a real jerk." It just doesn't happen that way.

People who wear smiles have a tendency to be fun, and who doesn't like to spend time with fun people? When selling, do all you can do to be the person at the sales party that people want to be around. You don't have to be the life of the party; you just need to be as competitive as possible in the smiling department. Smiles are a remarkable tool for knocking down the walls of apprehension in any situation.

The Perfect Handshake

"That guy almost took my hand off," were some of the sweetest words that fine evening in Bangor, Maine. This was the reaction from one of my finest customer's wife when one of my biggest competitor's sales reps introduced himself. He continued to squeeze her hand as if he were trying to squeeze the very last drop out of a mustard bottle. While most people just put a painful smile on and wait for the swelling to go down, this assertive woman would do no such thing. Let's just say she made him feel her pain. In the end, her pain was my company's gain.

Sales books for generations have been teaching the value of a deep, firm handshake and how it exudes confidence from the person delivering it. Be cautious…firm does not mean that you should act as if you are a human bench vise.

The limp-wristed handshake is equally annoying. In fact, American writer and editor William Allen White (1868–1944) once said this about former President Woodrow Wilson: "He has a handshake like a ten-cent pickled mackerel in brown paper."

While this pickled mackerel was not enough to keep Wilson out of the White House, it was enough to make a negative impression. Perception is reality, and if your customers' first thought when meeting you is a pickled mackerel, it is going to be awfully difficult to sell them something.

So what is the perfect handshake? It is one that is barely noticed by the person whose hand you are shaking. Because the handshake is only one part of the overall greeting process, you need to make sure it does not overpower your sincere smile, warm facial expression, interested tone of voice, and positive body language. Too much of one ingredient can screw up the perfect recipe.

When Things Go Wrong

Shit happens, right? Sometimes you have absolutely no control over some very important stuff that can make or break your best account. There will be times when it seems that nothing is going your way. This is when all of that trust and respect that you have earned from your customers will pay dividends. If they have little respect and trust for you, they will also have little patience when the fires flare up.

Don't Make Excuses

"Where the heart is willing it will find a thousand ways, but where it is unwilling it will find a thousand excuses."

—Indonesian proverb

Excuses are only speed bumps to progress. There is nothing worse than watching someone dance around the truth. If your company screws up, a colleague screws up, or you screw up, this too is a perfect time to be PRECISE. By this I mean you should say only what is necessary to make the problem disappear. Too often salespeople make problems worse by telling half-truths, passing blame, and by being too negative. They believe that if they look more ticked off than the customer about the problem, the customer will pass blame elsewhere.

News flash...it doesn't work. When problems arise, and you, a colleague, or your company dropped the ball, it is a perfect time to turn the challenge around and use it as an opportunity to gain even more respect and trust.

" It worked. We expressed remorse, asked for forgiveness and sales are up sixty percent. "

Long-term customers are smart enough to know that things will not always be rosy. So when the heat is on, you must:
- Address the challenge head-on
- Put more blame on yourself than on others
- Tell your customer that you will do everything you can to correct the problem
- Overdeliver on your promise
- *Never make excuses*

You will come out the other side with a better relationship than before the mix-up.

White Lies Are Risky

> "I should think it hardly possible to state the opposite of the truth with more precision."
>
> —Winston Churchill

Do you know anybody that has made "white-lying" a lifestyle? These people are so good at it that they start believing their own lies. In sales, as well as in life, once people can no longer trust what you say, your power to influence and positively affect them is reduced. So while it might seem like there are some short-term benefits to just a little white lie, it is the sum of these lies that can destroy your ability to be successful in sales. Once a customer no longer believes what you say, you are *done*. Don't ever risk it. It is better to be known as stupid, forgetful, idiotic, klutzy, and unorganized than it is to be known as a liar and a jackass.

Three Key PRECISE Phrases to Use on Every Scheduled Appointment

Okay, it's game time and you are about to have a meeting with a potential client. You have already performed Action #1—Prepare/have a specific objective, and are ready to greet your prospect as he walks into the conference room. If you remember anything in this chapter, make sure it includes this section. There are three specific things to say during Action #2 to earn respect and trust. These three things need to be preplanned, rehearsed, and repeated in every new scheduled appointment, be it in person or over the phone. (A scheduled appointment is one where the customers know that you are coming, have the defenses fully armed, and yet are willing to give you a shot at proving to them how you can make their lives better.)

To become the dominating, PRECISE, top performer in your company, you must read these phrases, practice them, and use them for 20 days. The three wall-crushing phrases sound like this (with key words in italics):

1. "*Thank you* for your time, Ms. _____."
2. "*I know* your *time* is important and you are probably in a hurry, so I would like to make our visit together as *quick* and as *valuable* as possible. I can do this by asking you a couple of *quick questions*."
3. "If *you believe* that we *might have a solution* for you, then we can discuss it in further detail. If not, I *thank you* for the opportunity."

This opening is designed to relieve pressure and to bring the customer's defenses down. Let's break it down piece by piece and tell you why it is so effective.

"Thank you for your time."

Many average sales reps don't even take time to thank their prospects or customers for giving them the opportunity to speak with them. They act like it is their God-given right to be in front of customers, when the customers are actually doing them a favor by taking time out of their busy day. When the PRECISE sales rep opens his discussion with these two magical words (*thank you*), he immediately sets himself apart from the average salesperson. These two words immediately help to break down the wall of apprehension that most customers bring with them into a sales call.

"I know your time is important . . ."

What do most customers think a sales rep is going to do during a scheduled appointment? If you answered, "Waste time by talking too much," you are correct. Because the PRECISE sales rep knows what 98 percent of all customers are thinking at the beginning of a sales call, she knows how to disarm them with this one rehearsed comment above. This simple fact that you are *acknowledging* the customers' time will put your customers' minds at ease. In essence, you are bringing up the time concern before they do, thereby disarming them.

"...quick and valuable..."

Because most customers are skeptics, they also think that most of what you are going to say will have little value to them. When you tell them that your intentions are to save them time and make every word valuable, the reaction from most customers is one of relief. When the customer is relieved, your chances of getting your message across are greatly improved.

"...quick questions..."

Can you see a trend developing here? Yes, we do use the word *quick* twice in our opening and that is by design. You want your customers to know that you plan to do your job effectively in the shortest time possible. When your customers realize that your questions are the vehicle that helps you save their time, they are much less apprehensive about letting you question them. In fact, they are much more eager to share the information that you need to better serve them because they now understand that it is in their best interest.

"If you believe..."

These three words let customers know that they are in control and that the buying decisions are theirs alone. Letting them know up front that their opinions and beliefs supersede yours as the salesperson will blow a big hole through the defenses.

"...might have a solution. If not, thank you..."

These words insinuate that you, as the salesperson, are not even sure if what you have is going to provide a solution to their needs. This lets them know that you have no plans to pressure them and removes yet another brick in the customer defense wall.

The Typical Customer Responses

While the customers' faces usually say, "Whew, amen, thank goodness this is not another sales schmuck," their lips usually say one of two things:

"Thank you for coming. Feel free to ask questions. Oh, and by the way, I am not in a hurry, so take your time."

"Thanks for coming. I appreciate your concern for my time, and I do only have seven minutes to chat."

Either response gives you valuable information. Isn't it useful to know in a sales call how much time you have to find a solution for your customers? This PRECISE opening pulls this information out of them much more softly than saying, "How much time do we have today?"

It is usually at this point during one of my seminars when a student raises her hand and says, "When I am in front of my customers, I know exactly how much time I have to get my point across." For those of you in similar situations I ask this: Imagine that you have an hour-long appointment scheduled with a sales rep that wanted to sell something to you. That rep comes in and tells you that his purpose is to have a specific and PRECISE discussion that will be done in half the time. Wouldn't that excite the hell out of you? Sure, it would! We all would like to spend a little less time with salespeople, wouldn't we?

So try this PRECISE opening, even if you have a specific amount of meeting time scheduled. When you use this PRECISE opening, it is like looking your customer in the eye and saying:

"Customer, I know you are thinking that I am about to bore the hell out of you and waste your time. I know you also think I'm going to ask you a bunch of questions that have almost no value to you. In fact, you think that because I am going to ask you a bunch of questions, what was already going to be a miserably long sales presentation is now going to be even longer. I know you are dying for me to just get to the point, show you what I have, and let you make an educated decision on your own. But frankly, I can't do that. Because the only way that I can make sure that I don't bore the hell out of you is by asking some quick and PRECISE questions. After asking these questions, I will then talk about only the benefits that you want to hear, and I will speak nothing of the features that you have no interest in. If after that you like what you hear and see, then we can move forward. If you do not like what you hear and see, I will not push you. In fact, I will pack up my bags and off I go. Oh, and did I mention that our conversation will take *half* the time of my competitor and you will learn *twice* as much?"

While I don't expect you to say the written words above, wouldn't it be nice to communicate a message such as this to a prospect before you present your solution? Well, you can with the less wordy and slightly more professional version listed before.

If you would like to change the wording up slightly, great, go ahead. Just make sure you use the key words listed in the PRECISE opening. Why? Because they work!

Curiosity Brings Walls Down While Prospecting

Respect and trust is difficult to build during a prospecting call. This is when customer's defenses are at their strongest, and when their inclination to becoming annoyed by salesperson is at its highest. Curiosity is the only weapon that a salesperson has at this point. Without creating curiosity, there is never an invitation to share more information. Without creating curiosity, the salesperson is just making an uninvited sales pitch that usually produces severe resistance.

When prospecting, your goal is to keep the sales game alive as long as possible. With curiosity as the foundation, the game will continue. Without it, you won't even get past the coin toss. Curiosity causes prospects to seek more information. When a prospect is seeking, they are not defending. And when they are on offense, it's tough to play defense. When this happens, those walls of resistance suddenly come down and the customer becomes more engaged. Remember what I said earlier: When prospects want, they are more willing to give. And the more willing they are to give, the more able you are to be PRECISE and deliver them the perfect solution. The next chapter will show you ways to build curiosity when prospecting.

PRECISE Action #2
Review

Respect and Trust

1. "*Thank you* for your time, Ms. _____."
2. "*I know your time* is important and you are probably in a hurry, so I would like to make our visit together as *quick* and as *valuable* as possible. I can do this by asking you a couple of *quick questions*."
3. "If *you believe* that *we might have a solution* for you, then we can discuss it in further detail. If not, I *thank you* for the opportunity."

Chapter Twelve

PRECISE Action #3: Engage Your Prospects with Questions and Curiosity—Till Death Do You Part

> Main Entry: engage (interest)
>
> Function: verb
>
> 1a: to interest someone in something and keep him thinking about it

There are some likenesses and some differences when engaging a cold prospect versus a warm prospect. A cold prospect is one that is not expecting you or your product or service. A warm prospect is someone that is expecting you and may or may not have already identified a need and a want. I will show you in this chapter exactly what to say in both cases.

Engage a Cold Prospect

As mentioned in the previous chapter, a cold prospect must be curious if the salesperson is to stay in the game. There are several ways to stir the interest of your prospect, however the best way to produce curiosity is by engaging your prospect with questions.

Ask an Engagement Question

"Leanne, uh, well, I really feel like I have gotten to know you, uh, and I, uh, think we have a lot in common. I was thinking maybe, you know, that you and I might, well, spend the rest of our lives together. Will ya?"

This is how I sounded when I asked my wife to marry me that cold December night in Rockefeller Center. And let me tell you, those words were anything but PRECISE. It's a good thing that woman kind of liked me, because if there was any doubt, I was in trouble.

When we are calling on cold prospects, I can assure you that they like us a lot less than my wife liked me on that night. She was enjoying my flapping around like a fish out of water while sounding like my tongue was frozen to my ice skates. While fiancées are willing to overlook the bumbling, cold prospects are not. Therefore, it is important to sound polished and PRECISE while using that perfect engagement question of our prospects. The objective of the question is as the definition states—to interest someone in something, and keep them thinking about it. Therefore, make sure that first question you use is one that "keeps them thinking about it," and creates a curiosity to hear more. If your question is flat, irrelevant, and inappropriate, and causes no curiosity, it will not be effective at pulling them closer to you and your solution.

While there are many types of engagement questions that you can use, I recommend that you find one or two that you like and stick with them. Remember, the best way to become consistently good at something is to do it or say it the same way each time. Like I said earlier, even though Tiger Woods can sink a putt between his legs and behind his back, he chooses not to, because that would decrease his chances of being successful.

The engagement question that I have found most successful is as follows:

> "Would you be interested in hearing how we can _____?"

Simply fill the blank in with the key benefit or benefits of the product or service that you are trying to sell. Some examples might be:
- Save you $142 a month?
- Save you 90 minutes a day?
- Give you peace of mind by increasing your coverage by $100K?
- Make you more efficient by helping you double your output?
- Help you become your company's top performer in 20 days or less? (That's mine)

The key here is to make sure that you are as specific as possible when filling in the blank. Make every attempt to have your _____ contain something tangible. Numbers and percentages help do this. Be PRECISE. Stay away from high-level, fluffy jargon.

Engage a Warm Prospect

Let's assume that you have already gone through Steps #1 (Prepare) and #2 (Respect and Trust) of the PRECISE Actions. You have prepared for the sales call and have all your materials out and ready. You have a set objective, and as a result, a way to measure your success in the call. The warm prospect has entered the room and the game has begun. You thanked her for her time and told her that you will save her time by asking a couple of quick questions. Warm prospects usually already have an idea about whom you are and what you sell. And there are usually reasons they let you through the door and have given you a chance at providing a solution.

Because this is the case, it makes sense for you to find out why they agreed to meet with you. While I don't expect you to say, "Why have you given me a shot at the title, oh Great Prospect?" there is an equally effective way of asking. We will lead with a Barbara Walters Question (see chapter 4). Once again, this question should be worded almost the same way each time. The only thing that will change is the product or service you fill in the _____. I like to ask my BW Question somewhat informally, and I ask it the same way each time regardless of the product or the customer.

> Salesperson: "What got you interested in taking a look at the _____?"

It is impressive how much information comes out of this one question. Your goal in asking any question is to find out what your customer is thinking and feeling and to gauge their interest in making a change or a new investment. Most often your warm prospect will tell you exactly why you are there. While they are telling you, grab that trusty pen and notepad and begin writing down as much as you can. What you write down are what I call BULLETS.

Look for Bullets

Bullets can be one, two, or perhaps three short words. In short, they are bullet points about the important things your customer has said.

The paragraph below is an example of a response that a customer might make to your BW Question. While you are reading, I would like you to write down in the space provided only the important information that you get from what you read. Write down no more than three connected words for each bullet. Remember, you are writing down only the bullets that will create your PRECISE presentation outline that will come later.

Engage Salesperson: "Nurse Mary, what got you interested in taking a look at the new PRECISE oral thermometer?"

Warm Prospect: "Currently, we are using glass thermometers. They take way too long to get a temperature. Our patients' jaws and teeth hurt after biting down on those things for two minutes, and on top of that, they are a pain to clean. I know we need something different, but I just don't know what. I saw one of your competitors yesterday, and that unit seemed easy to use, but it was pretty pricey."

Place your BULLETS here:

_____

_____

_____

_____

_____

How many BULLETS did you write down? If I had heard this from a prospect my BULLET notepad would have looked like this:

- Glass Thermometer
- Too Long
- Jaws/Teeth Hurt
- Pain to Clean
- (c) Easy Use
- (c) Pricey

Quick hint—Notice how I put a (c) next to the bullets that related to a competitive product.

This might seem like a lot to put on paper, but believe me it is doable. Your only challenge might be reading your own writing, as is the case with me.

So you might ask, "Do I need to write all the bullets down?" It all goes back to the photographic memory thing. If you have a good memory, then maybe you only have to write down a couple of bullets. If you are like me, and would rather not take the chance of not addressing something that is of concern to your prospect, then write down as much as you can. In either case, just be careful not to bury your head in your notepad so much that you become disengaged from your prospect.

Now I know you might be saying, "Sullivan, I don't think my prospects will spew bullets like the example above." If this is the case, it's okay, because the fun is just beginning. This was only our first try at engaging our customer with the hopes of gaining bullets.

Are They Spending Money Today?

It's good to know early on in a sales call if your prospect has already decided that they are going to make a change or an investment in a new solution. So when calling on a warm prospect make your second question a Fact-Finding Question like the ones listed.

Salesperson: "So Mrs. Prospect, have you decided . . .
- ...on the need for a product like this?"
- ...that you will definitely be making a change in the way you are doing things?"
- ...on investing in a newer system?"
- ...on changing suppliers?"
- ...on spending huge amounts of cash with my company?" (Maybe that's a bit overboard, but I think you get my point.)

In my seminars, I often hear from one or two audience members, "Oh boy, that seems awfully direct. It feels as if I am asking my prospect if they are ready to spend some money with me."

Guess what, *you are*. There is no W-I-M-P in the word PRECISE (okay, so there is an I and a P). If you hope to say as little as possible, waste nobody's time, and find the perfect solution for them, what's the risk in asking if they're serious about investing in a new solution? And when you ask the "if they plan to invest" question, you will often learn "when" they plan to invest. And if neither applies, they will tell you that they are just researching or "just looking around." Any one of these answers is great information.

Another one of my favorite seminar comments is "But Sullivan, that direct approach might work in New York City, but not where I live." My response to that is, "My friend, I have asked this PRECISE Question in the deepest parts of Kansas, Nebraska, and South Dakota and have lived to tell about it. We are not asking for their firstborn, we just want to know if they are kicking the tires or if the tire jack is already propped up."

Selling Need vs. Selling Your Solution

Customers will not buy your product or service unless you sell them on:

First—The *need* for a product or service like yours

Second—The *benefits* of your product or service

Therefore, it is important that you do not begin selling your solution until you convince them there is even a need for a product like yours. If they are already sold on the need and plan to make a change or a new investment, only then does it make sense to focus on your specific product or service offering.

The main reason you ask if they have already decided to make a change is because their answer dictates the direction of your next question and, in fact, your whole presentation.

You ask, "Have you decided that you are definitely making a change?"

The customer responds, "No, we have not decided if we need to spend the money. We are just looking at our options right now."

If this is the response you get, don't begin telling them how great your product is. Your product can be the greatest in its class, but it won't matter if they don't see a need. Selling the need for your product is entirely different than selling your product itself. At this point, you must sell the need before selling the specifics of your solution. Regardless of selling need or selling the product, it's necessary to use the questioning skills we discussed earlier in the book. The when, where and in what order do you use these questions will be discussed shortly.

> Make sure they are sold on their need before they are sold on your product.

In the next chapter, I will give you a questioning sequence that will not insult or bore your customer. It also won't look like a blueprint to a computer microchip. Instead, you'll find it easy to remember and versatile enough to use in most every selling situation. Chapter 14 is worth $10,000 to you.

Chapter Thirteen

CLEAR Questioning: The $10,000 Questioning Technique That You Get Free With This Book

Have you ever sat through a sales meeting that was given by a marketing guru or some other sales expert where they gave you a list of what they call "probing questions"? I don't know about you, but when I'm being sold to, I certainly don't want any salespeople probing me. Only one person probes me, and that's my internal medicine doctor. Having said that, what always drove me nuts about the list of new product training probing questions was there was no specific order, and they were impossible to remember.

I remember during the early nineties when I was learning about one of our newest products, a product manager was reviewing the *long list* of *probing questions* that I needed to ask to get my prospects interested. The product I was promoting was a prober itself (yep, here we go with that colonoscope again). The manager took his transparency (of course, this was pre-PowerPoint days), ruffled it around a few times, flipped it upside down, then sideways and reviewed the questions. When I saw this list, I thought I was being shown the blueprints to the space shuttle. It contained boxes, bars, and highlighted text of all shapes and colors. He called it a flowchart, but to me it was hieroglyphics that I could never remember.

Typical Probing Question techniques that are taught in sales books are rarely adopted and repeatedly used in the field. Most of them do a fine job of discussing the importance of questioning but leave too much to the imagination about how to use those questions. It is like a football player being coached on the fundamentals but never being told when and in what situation he is supposed to use them. It would not be a good thing if a player were tackling when he should be blocking or blocking when he should be tackling. Nor would it be a good thing if that player was coached on how to punt the ball but never told that he probably shouldn't be doing it on first down.

The Playbook

Well my friend, the playbook has just arrived and it's all yours. You now have the secret weapon to winning the game. We have already discussed the blocking and tackling of PRECISE Selling, now I will give you the $10,000 technique that will get you to the Super Bowl. It is called CLEAR Questioning, because that's exactly what it is. According to Merriam-Webster, "clear" means quickly and easily understood. It also implies freedom from obscurity, ambiguity, or undue complexity. That's what CLEAR Questioning is. It is clear and easy to remember and repeat regardless of the selling situation or the size of the selling opportunity. It is CLEAR to use whether you are selling on the phone or in person. It doesn't matter if you are selling high-tech telecommunications equipment worth $1 million a pop, selling pharmaceuticals to clinics and hospitals, or selling DVD players for an electronics store, this line of questioning just makes sense.

Once you learn and remember CLEAR questioning (which should take about three minutes), your mind will fire at the perfect time in your sales calls. Let's imagine your PRECISE sales call. You have already prepared all your materials and set an objective (P). You have built respect and trust by thanking them (R). You have engaged them with questions and curiosity (E). And now it is time to engage them further with CLEAR.

What does CLEAR stand for?
C—Currently
L—Looked
E—Effective/Enjoy
A—Alter
R—Responsible for Decisions

C = CURRENTLY— (CLEAR)

> What product/company/solution are you currently using?

Doesn't it make sense to find out your prospect's current circumstances and who or what company they have been doing business with? They may be miserable with their current product, supplier, or service company, or they may be in love with them. Either way, it's necessary to know who and what they are. Sales instructor gurus all over the world love to psychoanalyze what goes on in a sale but it really is simple. Your solution needs to make your prospect's life better than it currently is. If you don't even know what their current situation is, how will you ever know if you can do better? This question will let you know what you are up against and the information gained from it will be important in designing your presentation that is to come later. I am awestruck when I see salespeople begin a presentation or demonstration on their solution without ever asking this question.

L= LOOKED — (CLEAR)

> Have you looked at any newer technology…similar system…other solutions? (pick one)

This question will get you two bits of information. Are they serious about investing or buying or changing products or suppliers?

If so, which competitor do you need to be better than?

For several years, I failed to coach salespeople on this important question. As a result, some sales reps were doing excellent presentations about how their solution would be better than what the prospect was currently using. All along they were neglecting to address how their product was better than other solutions presently available on the market.

If your competition has already proven that their solution is better than what the prospect currently uses, then you have to switch gears a little. You will not focus your presentation on bettering their old solution but on bettering the current competition that they may have already researched and learned about.

For example, let's say you sold cars for a living and a customer walks in the showroom. You warmly greet them, thank them for stopping by, and tell them you want to save them time by asking a couple quick questions. You then ask an engagement question or two and then go to CLEAR Questioning.

You: "So Joe, what are you currently driving?"

Prospect: "A 1968 Dodge Dart."

The average sales rep might assume too much at that point and say, "Wooo, time to take a little stroll to the used car lot. I think we can upgrade you to the 1977 El Camino."

The PRECISE rep, on the other hand, continues with the next question:

You: "Have you looked at or driven any newer cars recently?"

Prospect: "As a matter of fact, we just won the Powerball and have a little extra cash in our pocket. We just test-drove a Lamborghini, and we really think that baby is a nice ride."

Can you see how the "looked" prevented you from trying to compare your cars to what they have now and changed your frame of reference? This is why this question is so important. Believe me, I tried to sell against a few "1968 Dodge Darts" myself when I should have been selling against the Lamborghini. In the end, they bought the Lamborghini instead of the '77 El Camino.

E=EFFECTIVE/ENJOY— (CL_EAR)

> What makes your current supplier so effective?
>
> *or*
>
> What is so effective about the product you currently use?
>
> *or*
>
> What do you enjoy about that system?

Once your (L) question lets you know if you are going to be comparing your solution to what they currently use or to what they most recently have seen, it's time to find out what they find effective or enjoy about it. The (E)ffective Question is one seldom used by the average rep but is just as important as asking what the prospect is unhappy with. Your eventual goal in providing any solution is to heal the pain where your customer hurts without creating pain in another area where they don't hurt. So by asking what they find effective about how they do things now, you get a great idea about what is important to them.

Despite how valuable it is in helping find the right solution for their prospect, many average sales reps shy away from the (E)ffective Question. They feel there is a risk in getting the prospect to think about what they specifically like about their current solution. They think, "I want to find out where they are hurting, not where they are happy. They don't need to be think of reasons to stay with their current solution."

My lovely wife was once a sales rep for a large and well-known pharmaceutical company. This company had a large training department and invested tens of thousands of dollars on new hires. While they were heavy on PIC Knowledge, they were light on selling skills. During one of the early weeks in the field, my wife was traveling with her regional manager. At this point, I had already brainwashed Leanne with PRECISE Selling and sent her out the door fired up and feeling confident. She rehearsed and polished her presentation and knew what questions to use to engage her prospect.

Time had come for her to hit the field with her boss. Leanne's territory was a large chunk of the south side of Chicago. She was a little anxious about her first day, so we reviewed her selling skills and spent a little time on how to be the "animal" by matching her customer. Leanne, who grew up in Kansas City, did not have the best south-side accent so I popped in an old *Saturday Night Live* videotape and made her review it several times.

Say it with me Leanne, "Daa Bears, daa Blackhawks, daa sinusitis, Daa drugs." After looking at me like I was the one on drugs, she jumped in her fancy Ford Taurus and off she went. Then came her first call at a large family practice clinic. As she approached her first doctor in the hallway, she was ready to be PRECISE. Her manager was about to see Dana Carnegie in action. She was prepared, broke down the walls, and got permission to ask a few questions. She asked what drug her doctor prospect was currently using to treat chronic sinusitis. She then followed by asking if he had looked at some of the newer antibiotics on the market that were even more effective with fewer side effects. That question was followed with one inquiring about what he found effective about that drug. The doctor opened up like a bank vault and she diligently took notes. "This PRECISE stuff is working," she thought. "My husband isn't such an idiot after all."

After chatting with the doctor for several minutes and getting a commitment to prescribe her product, she was elated. That is, until she got out in the car and was reprimanded by her manager.

He said, "What was that?"

She proceeded to rat me out and tell him that her husband taught this stuff.

He said, "Great, but you are told in training that your number one objective is to read the package insert of your drug to your customer. You only have five minutes with these doctors and they need to know as much as possible about your product in that time frame. And why on earth were you asking him what he found effective about the drugs he is prescribing now?"

He might as well have said, "Leanne, your objective is to fire off as much meaningless detail as possible while wasting as much of your prospect's time as possible.

After that day, Leanne had two types of selling skills. One that made her customers happy, and one that made her manager happy.

Use What They Love Against Them

What happens if the prospect sees no need for a change and is satisfied with their current solution? What if they think there is nothing wrong with the way things are done now? Ever face one of these situations? Hello…we do every day.

In his book, *Why We Buy,* self-described retail anthropologist Paco Underhill notes that if consumers bought only what they really needed, and spent money only when they had problems with what they currently used, the economy would collapse. You don't want that to happen now, do you? So it is your responsibility to take what they enjoy and find effective and use it against them to create a want.

They might tell you they love the comfort of the velour seats in their Chevy Impala, but wait until they hear about your new and improved "pleather." You would only get this information if you asked what they enjoyed. You would only tell them about your "pleather" if you knew that seat comfort was important to them. Can you see how asking sets you up to sell your story?

The PRECISE sales rep is not negatively affected when prospects start spewing all the features they love about their current supplier or product. The PRECISE rep just sits back, listens patiently, and takes notes on what they specifically enjoy. These notes become bullets. Bullets become what you will base your presentation on. The more they find effective and enjoy about what they are currently using, the more bullets you have. This is a good thing! You just need to convince them in ACTION #4 (Convey Solution) that although they are satisfied in those areas, you intend to show them how they can be even happier! We will get to that later.

Let's try a bullet exercise again. I will write an excerpt from a sales call, and I want you to identify the bullets (one, two, or three words to write on your notepad that will become your sales PRECISE outline).

In this example, let's say you are a telecommunications rep that sells everything from batteries to high-end computer servers to small businesses. You are trying to become the preferred supplier and service agent to Precision Widgets. You have already gone through your Prepare and Respect and Trust Actions, asked some engagement questions and asked the C and T questions. You then ask:

You: "You mentioned you use XYZ Telecom and have not looked at alternative suppliers since you switched to them five years ago. It sounds like they have done a good job for you. What makes them so effective?"

Prospect: "They've been good. They get me what I need three days after I contact them. And the sales rep usually gets back to me within twenty-four hours if he can. Also, he stops by here once a month to check on things."

You: "Is there anything else they do effectively?"

Prospect: "Well, they let me fax my orders in, which is nice. Although sometimes the line is busy, which can be a hassle."

Now review the dialogue again and write down the bullets in the space provided.

_____

_____

_____

_____

_____

Notice how this PRECISE rep tried to pull as much information as possible out of the prospect with the question, "Is there anything else?" This will make them think a bit. The more they think, the more inside their heads and hearts you get.

Another note! While your prospect is sharing information, it is important that you resist your temptation to jump in and start selling.

> The "Engage with Questions and Curiosity Action" is all about getting information in bundles, not about addressing each point as they come up.

Now let's review your bullets that you wrote down on the last page. Did they look something like this?

- 3-day service
- 24-hour service
- 1 visit/month
- Fax order hassles

If what you wrote resembles this nice job. Remember that you have to find a balance between getting those bullets on that notepad vs. burying your head and disengaging your prospect. I prefer to err on the side of getting more notes. If your objective is to serve your prospect and to find the right solution for them, it is most important that you have those bullets written down.

A=ALTER—(CLEAR)

> Is there anything that you would alter about the way your current supplier services you?
>
> *or*
>
> Is there anything you would alter about the functionality of your current product?

The information that you get from this question is often the most valuable. The (A)lter Question is used to find out where your prospect is hurting. The hope is that they will fire off five or six problems they have, you jot down the bullets, and then convey your solution. But as you know, it does not always happen this way. Sometimes they share many (E)ffective Bullets and few (A)lter Bullets. Who cares!

> Don't discriminate. Love all bullets equally.

A bullet is a bullet. Bullets are the secret combination to unlock the mind and heart of your prospect. When you get bullets, you are getting the ingredients to a successful sale.

It is as if the prospect is telling you, "Focus on these benefits, and you will keep me interested, build my curiosity, and convince me that you can fix the problems I hate, without sacrificing the features I like. If you shy too far away from those bullets, you will bore the hell out of me and waste my time."

Help Them Help You with Floating Bullets

What happens when you have a tight-lipped prospect that doesn't share information freely? You ask an (E) and an (A) Question, and they barely move their lips. This usually happens if you have not been successful in bringing down the customer's defenses and began building respect and trust. It also happens often when you don't tell the prospect that you will be asking a couple of timesaving questions to make the sale go as quickly and painlessly as possible.

There are those times, however, when the walls just don't come down. To prevent this, and to lead your prospect to the specific topics that you want to stress about your solution, you can add a few bullets of your own to the end of your question. The hope is that they will grab onto a topic you want to discuss and inadvertently give you permission to go there. You will more often do this when asking the (A)lter Question.

For instance, let's say that your product is much faster and much easier to service than the product or service your prospect currently uses. These are obviously two features that you would like to make part of your presentation. But you want them to tell you it is important, not you to tell them. Remember what we said about the contrarian nature of people. Tell them speed and service is essential and their tendency is to minimize its importance or disagree (because they didn't come up with it, you did; you don't want that). A good way to avoid this while leading your prospect to the bullets you want to discuss is by using your (A)lter questioning with a Floating Bullet Add-On. An example is:

"Is there anything that you would alter about the way your current system is working, whether it be slow speed, performance, or perhaps any service concerns?"

This (A)lter Question with the Floating Bullet Add-On still allows your prospect the opportunity to come up with their own bullets, but at the same time leads them to bullets you would like to discuss. Remember, the supreme objective is to get as many bullets as possible. The most comprehensive bullet list is one that contains topics that they say are important. It doesn't matter if they thought of it themselves, or if they agreed with the importance of the ones that you lead them to. The objective is to build the bulleted outline for the presentation that you will deliver later.

R=Responsible—(CLEA**R**)

Who, as well as yourself, is responsible for deciding about_____?
(insert what you do or sell)

Have you ever delivered your finest sales presentation to somebody who has absolutely no decision-making responsibility whatsoever? I have. By asking early on in your sales call, you can prevent this from happening. It can also prevent you from wasting your time and get you the needed information to get in front of the right prospects that can make things happen. And don't assume that you know the answer to this question. In this complex business environment that we live in, change in decision-makers is certain. I have seen more than a few accounts lost because the decision-makers had changed, and the sales reps had no clue because they thought they already knew. Make a habit of asking this question every time you are presenting a solution to a new prospect or a current customer.

Another reason to ask this question is to put some responsibility on the prospect. If they tell you that they do have a say in choosing a solution, when you ask for the order it will be more difficult for them to stall and to misinform. They will feel more obliged to either make a decision, or be more honest about who does. Either way, by asking the (R)esponsible Question early on, you will waste little time and get to the right people much earlier.

"...as well as yourself..."

Notice the wording in the (R) Question. When you ask, "Who as well as yourself...," you are making your prospect feel important, even if he is not. This itself does a nice job of breaking down the walls. If he is a decision-maker, then you gave him the respect he wants. If he is not, he will be so thankful for the respect you showed him that he is often more than willing to throw others "under the bus" and share exactly how decisions are made. It's a nice little game of give and take. You give respect, and they give you the names of three other people that you *really* need to get with.

"I Already Ask Questions Like These... Most of the Time."

I often hear this from students in my seminars. My response is usually, "Would it be better if you did it all the time?" When I sell, I stick to CLEAR on almost every situation. Why? Because it's easy to remember and gets me the information I need to be PRECISE. It carries out the goal of getting the customer to tell me what it will take to come up with the perfect solution and allows me to lead them to the benefits I want to discuss.

I used to get hung up on CLEAR and insist the salespeople I coached stick as close to the verbiage as possible. My thoughts were that if I allowed too much room for "freestyling," my students would go right back to selling the way they used to. While I may have softened a bit, I do believe the best way to be effective is to ask these questions in a repeatable manner. "Repeatable manner" is a fancy way of saying, "Say it the same way each time," regardless of the order. If you find that instead of CLEAR questions you would rather switch up the order and ask RAELC questions…go nuts! But ask RAELC questions each time. Be the best at asking RAELC questions. Hell, come up with your own fancy acronym. Just stick to it.

The goal here is to keep your questions repeatable, memorable, and sustainable. Can Tiger Woods sink a putt between his legs or behind his back on Sunday? Sure he could. But he strokes the putt the same way each time because it increases his chances for success. Be a Tiger and use the power of repetition.

PRECISE Action #3
Review

Engage with Questions and Curiosity

Cold Prospect—"Would you be interested in hearing how we can_____?"

Warm Prospect

- "What got you interested?"
- "Have you already decided on the need for a product like this?"

C – "What are you currently using?"

L – "Have you looked at any newer technology°similar systems°other solutions?" (Pick One)

E – "What do you find effective or enjoy about what you currently use?"

A – "What would you alter about the way you are doing things now?"

R –"Who, in addition to yourself, is responsible for making decisions?"

Make notes on the bullets your prospect gave you.

Chapter Fourteen
PRECISE Action #4: Convey Your Solution Using Smart Bombs, Not Dumb Bombs

Main Entry: con·vey

Function: verb

1a: to bear from one place to another; especially: to move in a continuous stream or mass

1b: to impart or communicate by statement, suggestion, gesture, appearance or questions!

—Sullivan Unabridged Dictionary

The seven PRECISE Actions move quickly. Once you have gained at least three bullets as a result of your Engage with Questions and Curiosity Action, and feel confident that you have enough information to design a customized presentation, it is then time to Convey Solution. To convey means to bear from one place to another, and that's exactly what happens at this point. You move out of the main questioning action and into more of the traditional presentation. This is the part of a sales call that salespeople love the most, and it is where the average sales rep feels most confident. Why is that? Because most sales reps love to talk about their solution, and this is the part of the call that allows them to move their lips more than any other step in the PRECISE Actions. Be careful however. This is not a hall pass to start firing worthless features and benefits.

Be a Precision-Guided Weapon, Not a Dumb Bomb

Large bombers have been a staple in the American military since World War II. As we turn on the Discovery Channel we see old footage of these aircraft dropping "dumb bomb" after "dumb bomb" over the skies of Germany, Japan, and Vietnam. This "carpet bombing" was the only way to ensure the mission was accomplished. However, there was much collateral damage done in the process. In modern military times, there are now weapons known as smart bombs. The goal of these smart bombs is to engage the target, use only enough ordinances as needed, and be as PRECISE as possible to carry out the mission. They hit more targets with less weapons.

In sales, you too need to be a smart bomb. While your competition is dropping masses of "dumb bombs" in the form of statements about features, benefits, bells and whistles, you can operate as a precision-guided weapon. By focusing your presentation only on those bullets that you uncovered during the Engage with Questions Action, your customer will hang on your every word.

The Transition to the Solution

To smoothly move into the Convey Solution step of your PRECISE Actions, you need an effective transition. The most effective way to do this is with a rehearsed sentence or two that you feel comfortable with. One example might be as follows:

> "Mr. Gates, from what you told me, I believe we can provide some solutions to some of the challenges that you are having with your current product/solution/supplier. In addition, I think we can even improve on some of the features that you were satisfied with in regards to your current product. Let's take a look."

I have been using this transition on almost every sales presentation that I have made over the past seven years. It is rehearsed, and therefore it does not sound canned or "salesy." This transition does a great job of moving us from one step of the sales actions, Engage with Questions, right into our Convey Solution step with confidence.

Curiosity

Reread the transition statement above and play customer for a moment. How would you feel if a sales rep took the time to question you about your wants and needs, and then really listened to what you were saying? What if he then confidently suggested to you that he has a solution to your problems and can provide that solution without you having to sacrifice the features that you were currently satisfied with your current product? The answer I most often get in my seminars is *curious*; curious to see if that sales rep's product can really do all he said it could.

If this is how you felt as the customer, then the sales rep has carried out her mission of making you curious and more interested in what she is about to say. It is difficult to stir emotion, activity, and interest without throwing curiosity into the sales mix.

The transition above shows confidence in your product and creates customer curiosity. This curiosity creates an invitation for you to deliver more details about the benefits of your solution. Curiosity causes prospects to seek more information. When a prospect is seeking, they are not defending. The walls of resistance suddenly come down and the customer becomes more engaged.

> When prospects want, they are more willing to give.

And the more willing they are to give, the more able you are to be PRECISE and deliver the perfect solution.

Tell Them Who You Are

If the prospect is not familiar with your company, it is important that you take a few seconds to tell them. Do not give them a thirty-minute PowerPoint presentation about how your company was founded during the Great Depression unless that story will help build respect and trust. Also, don't become a B-52 bomber and start dropping a canned sales presentation on their heads. A little history is all we are looking for here. If what you are saying does not help you gain credibility, respect, and trust, then save it. I recommend that you come up with a verbal commercial consisting of two or three precise sentences. Practice your commercial like an actor would practice his lines—so you say it smoothly and with confidence.

Load the Bullets and Shoot

Your next step is to hit your bullets. Grab your notepad and start from the hot bullet. This is the bullet that you believe will have the most immediate impact. For instance, let's say that your prospect told you that they wasted much time returning damaged product back to their current supplier. You take this information and turn it into the bullet "Quality/Time." If your company produces high-quality products (and that is a main benefit of doing business with you), then start your Convey Solution Action with that topic. Or if this is the #1 concern of your prospect, and you believe your product or service will provide a solution, then make that topic your hot bullet. Either way, you want the most "bang for your buck" immediately, so start with the bullet that carries with it the most interest.

Your notepad might look like this:

• 3-day service
• 24-hour response
• Quality/time
• Fax order hassles

Each Bullet Gets Its Own Presentation

To effectively convey your solution, you must do an individual presentation on each bullet separately. Most salespeople (if they have even gotten this far in the sales process) often roll all the bullets into one large presentation. Instead, the PRECISE sales rep attacks each topic separately, opens a discussion, explains why his solution is better, and then gets an agreement on each bullet before going on to the next.

These little "yeses" and minor agreements build emotion and confirm the level of interest the prospect has and does it at a nice, gradual pace. Customers want a smooth ride…not one that will give them whiplash. And later, when you ask for the order, your request for minor agreements will have already primed them for the big request. When this happens, it will not seem as if you just put the "pedal to the metal." On the contrary, their momentum will already be carrying them toward the final destination. It will now just take a little nonthreatening tap on the gas pedal to get them to make the big commitment.

Question Until They Feel the Pain

When a prospect shares an (A)lter bullet with you, they are obviously feeling some pain. It is now time to turn that hot bullet into a very painful white-hot bullet. To increase that pain and to get even deeper into their head and heart it is helpful to question further. Consequence Questions are helpful in achieving this objective. These are questions that help the prospect share the impact of the problems they are having. It is not enough to know that somebody is having quality issues as in the example above. You need to find out the consequences of those quality issues while getting them to "feel the pain" that comes with those consequences all over again. This is where you can make the most impact in your presentation. An example might sound like this:

> "I would like to begin my presentation by showing you how my company's twelve-point quality manufacturing process might be able to give you back some of those hours that you may be losing. But first, can you tell me what have been the negative consequences resulting from poor quality."

Notice how the first sentence creates curiosity and shows the confidence you have in your solution. Also, notice how the Consequence Question (…what have been the negative consequences…) tries to get the prospect to elaborate more on the "pain."

Get Agreement, Then Check Off the Bullet

After doing a "little presentation" on how your solution can relieve your customer's pain, get some agreement from the customer that you provided the correct medicine. Never move on to another bullet until you have gotten an agreement on the bullet you just addressed. Ask a question like:

> PRECISE Rep: "Can you see how our emphasis on total quality manufacturing with our twelve-point quality check will save you the added labor costs that you may be spending now?"
> Prospect: "Yes, I like your process. It could save us some money."

• 3-day service	
• 24-hour response	
~~Quality/time~~	
• Fax order hassles	

At this point, grab that pen of yours and draw a line through the bullet that you just addressed. Congratulations, you now have one minor agreement and the "sales car" is on the move. Now go to the next hot bullet, load it up, and do another individual presentation. Remember to ask a Consequence Question to get the prospect thinking more about the real problems associated with their unhappiness. Once they feel the pain, give them your medicine, and ask them how they like it.

Benefits Make the Bullet More Powerful

"Features and benefits" is a common phrase used in sales. In the PRECISE Sales World, we do things a little differently. Therefore, we don't talk about features and benefits; we talk about benefits then features. Average sales reps have no problem discussing the features of their solution. Features are usually easy to find on a brochure, easy to remember, and easy to spew. Changing salespeople from B-52 feature bombers to PRECISE benefit dropping machines is not easy. It takes a fundamental change away from what most salespeople are comfortable with. A trick to being PRECISE is to get to the benefit before you get to the feature.

Let's show an example:

You sell big screen televisions for a living, and your company has the finest selection of wide-screen, HDTV bad boys that any sports-loving freak could find. A prospect walks in the door, and you go through PRECISE Actions (P), (R), and (E). You get some topics to focus on and write down a few hot bullets. Your prospect tells you their current TV was too small for the room they live in.

The average sales rep readies the payload and begins dropping bombs:

"We have the perfect TV for you. It is sixty inches, diagonal, and is HDTV ready. It can be wired for stereo surround sound and has picture-in-picture. Just look at that baby. She's a beaut!"

While I love this rep's enthusiasm for his product, he is just feature dropping. He did not mention one benefit in his presentation. There is a better way.

The PRECISE Rep takes the benefit approach. After asking a few Consequence Questions, he then conveys his solution:

"You mentioned that your eyes are not what they used to be. I believe we have the perfect TV to suit your needs. It will allow you to watch comfortably from any couch in the room (benefit). It will also lessen the strain on your eyes (benefit) and as a result allow you to watch college football from 11:00 a.m. until 11:00 p.m. (this benefit would get me). In addition, our TV will make you feel as if you are actually playing in the game (benefit). You will feel like Randy Moss (benefit...I think) catching a pass while focusing on the rotation of the tightest spiral passes coming right through your screen (benefit). We provide this vivid clarity (benefit) with our HDTV tuner (feature) developed specifically for our large sixty-inch PRECISE LT Pro TV."

Notice how the PRECISE sales rep presents the benefits first and the features second. Stating them first makes them top priority; and that's exactly what they should be. Oh, don't worry. You will get to the features. Just lead with the benefits and the feature will be close behind. But lead with a feature, and watch how easily the benefit gets lost. Benefits are much more temperamental and need spoiling. Don't neglect them. They are the defense against customer confusion and boredom.

HDTHMP Will Bring Out the Benefit

Why should somebody get involved in your product, company, or solution? Go ahead; take twenty seconds to think about it. Was the answer you gave a benefit or a feature? You will know you have arrived at the benefit only when you can no longer answer the following question:

"How does that help my prospect?"

Keep going until you get to something that sounds almost too basic. The TV example would look like this. The feature is:

• Sixty-inch screen

"How does that help my prospect?" The image is incredibly large.

"How does that help my prospect?" He doesn't have to squint.

"How does that help my prospect?" He can watch more TV, more comfortably.

"How does that help my prospect?" I don't know...I've had enough!

Okay, by continuing to ask yourself HDTHMP, you have arrived at the benefit. If you are doing a presentation on a sixty-inch big screen TV, you will want to start your presentation from the bottom up. So it sounds like this:

"Mr. Prospect, you will be able to watch more TV, more comfortably (4), and you will not have to squint while doing it (3). And this is all done with an incredibly large image (2) projected from our sixty-inch big screen TV (1)."

Try this exercise with your products or services and keep asking yourself, "How does that help my prospect?" This example only drills down four steps, but you may be surprised when you try this exercise with your product or service. In my seminars, I find most students end up digging down deep, and it often takes a bunch of "HDTHMPs" before they get to the core benefit.

Different Benefits for Different Buyers

There are many different types of buyers that you will sell to. Different benefits must be communicated to these different prospects. The higher up the decision-making ladder you go, the more important your delivery of benefits becomes. The leaders in the executive suite like to cut through the crap and get right to the benefits of your solution. These "chief" types usually have risen to their positions because they are PRECISE. So to get the executive to open up, you too need to be PRECISE. Being PRECISE means spending more time on benefits than on features. If you are busy firing feature after feature at the CEO, you will not only bore her, but you risk never having an audience at that level again.

The further down the decision-making ladder you go, the more you can get away with feature dropping. But just because the consequences are not as severe, this does not mean it should be done. Before any sales call, think of the features that you might find yourself discussing with your prospect. Then ask a few HDTHMPs. By thinking of them before the call, you will be more apt to focus on them during the call.

Be the Great Gazoo

Fred Flintstone was one of my favorite cartoon characters when I was a child (maybe because I am shaped like him). For those of you that are familiar with Fred, you might remember the small two-foot, green space alien known as the Great Gazoo that would occasionally show up and park himself on Fred Flintstone's shoulder. Well, when demonstrating your product or service, there will be times when customers would rather turn their attention away from you and toward either the solution you are demonstrating or your brochure. It is at this point when you will let your customers figure some stuff out on their own. When they do this, look at yourself as the barely visible Little Green Man sitting on your customer's shoulder. At this point, your only job is to help solidify and verbalize some of the thoughts that they may be thinking.

This is the perfect time to use Little Yes Questions. Remember those? Those are the ones that are statements that end with a question and include phrases such as:

...couldn't it? *or*...couldn't you?

...shouldn't it? *or*...shouldn't you?

...wouldn't it? *or*...wouldn't you?

...isn't it? *or* ...aren't you?

Let's say the prospect just picked up your product and quickly and easily got it to work. You might say subtly, "The product seems easy to use, doesn't it?"

Or perhaps some prospects just looked at a financial analysis of using your service, and their eyes lit up like Christmas trees. You might say, "Saving several hundred dollars a month using our service would help increase cash flow, wouldn't it?" This is all done while their attention is focused away from you and onto your solution.

While these Little Yes Questions are effective, be careful not to overdo it. While it is effective to get "Little Yeses," you do not want to sound patronizing.

Don't Overdo the Statistics

> "He used statistics the way a drunkard uses lampposts—
> for support, not illumination."
>
> —Andrew Lang

Be careful using numbers and statistics unless they directly support the benefit that you are "selling." And don't use them as an "I told you so." Use them only to strengthen your argument. And while you are pulling out those percentages, show enthusiasm about your proof. While stats can sometimes be boring, your energy and enthusiasm can make them more interesting and believable.

Know your audience. Some prospects, depending on their positions, get all giddy with bubble graphs and flowcharts. If this is the case, then give them as much as they need. But don't torture those that have no interest. There is little worse than hearing a sales rep use numbers and facts that do nothing to "illuminate" the presentation. Always think of your audience before spewing numbers, and don't forget that being PRECISE means saying only what is necessary to inform and excite your prospect.

> "Before I came here I was confused about this subject. Having listened to your lecture I am still confused. But on a higher level."
>
> —Enrico Fermi (1901–1954), Italian physicist

I have seen many "technical salespeople" confuse the hell out of prospects because they delivered a "canned" presentation designed to be delivered to a more technical audience. Before you launch into your "lecture," remember to question first to find out your prospect's level of expertise. Then match your presentation to that level of expertise.

How Testimonials Just Plain Work

If you have ever read a book on sales, then you have no doubt read about the value of testimonial letters. Testimonial letters, written by happy customers, consist of just a few sentences or paragraphs that tell prospects why you, your company, and your product or service are so damn good. These testimonial letters do a super job of giving you and your company credibility. When presenting your company or solution, you should carry with you at least three testimonial letters from happy users.

Throughout my career the products that I have been most successful selling were also the ones that had the most testimonials backing them up. My most successful product of all time was like an out-of-control freight train. It was an $11,000 scope, and I sold lots of them. Early on, I decided that I was going to get as many testimonial letters from happy users as possible. To do this, my objective was to get one testimonial letter for every three happy users. As I began to sell more products, I began to get more testimonial letters. The more testimonial letters I got, the more sales I began to get. And this pattern continued until I led the company in the sales of that product.

In the end, I had over thirty-five letters from happy customers. These letters were from many different types of users that were happy about many different things. There were doctors that were happy about the performance of the scope. There were nurses that found the scope easy to maintain. There were medical assistants that found the scope easy to clean. There were office managers who could not believe the price of the scope and saw great value in it. And there were patients that found some value in being able to see the results of an exam in real-time.

I had all of these letters in my presentation binder, ready to pull out at a second's notice. When a medical assistant would bring up a concern about the cleaning of the scope, I would pull out the two or three letters from other medical assistants. These letters would say that these current users also had concerns at first, but were now convinced that what I had said in my presentation was true. When a nurse would tell me that they were concerned about the maintenance of the scope, I would pull out three or four letters from nurses that once felt the same way, but were now happy.

These letters were gold. I can't tell you how many times these things pulled my sale back from the abyss and turned the prospect completely around. They often gave me credibility I could find nowhere else. They were like having a hundred or more medical professionals standing in the bullpen waiting for me to call them out at a seconds notice to back up everything I was saying.

How Do I Get Testimonial Letters?

First, you need to plan to get testimonial letters. Set an objective to get it done. Remember, the more you have, the more credibility you have—so don't skimp here. To make sure you don't neglect this step, you should make time in your daily planner or PDA to follow up with recent customers. They will appreciate your follow up and that you are checking to see that all is well. If all is well, they will usually be willing to share their positive experiences in writing. I usually like to help them in the writing of the letter by asking, "What is it that you like about the product? How is it making your life easier?"

Once they tell me, I then ask if we can put those specific points on paper so I could share them, if need be, with other interested customers. You will be amazed at how easy this is.

If they like you and what your company has done for them, this should be a piece of cake. If they agree to do it, but are strapped for time, offer to take the words that they just said and put them on paper yourself. If they agree with what they see, ask for permission to put it on their letterhead, and then put it into your presentation binder.

Here is how I ask.

"Dr. Allan, I often have interested physicians that would like to talk to a colleague to get their opinions on how our product and company have performed. I know you have a busy practice and have little time to jump on the phone during the day. Would it be okay if you just put your thoughts in writing? This way, when doctors ask if they can call you, I can quickly let them know your opinion without them interrupting your day."

If I ever sense any reluctance, or feel like I am annoying the hell out of them, I back off. The following is an example of a testimonial letter that has been responsible for some sales.

A Testimonial Letter That Works

Allan Family Medical Practice
November 14, 2003

Dr. James Allan
21 Maple Street
Shelbina, Missouri 63468

Dear Brian,

This is just a brief note to express our satisfaction with your Automatic Blood Pressure Monitor, and our thanks for continuing to provide service and new and improved products. The monitor saves our staff time, which in turn saves the practice and patients money. We had the privilege of being a beta test site for your new software for the device, and let me say we are excited about this new and improved version of the software. Your company's attention to detail and customer satisfaction continues to impress us, and we look forward to continuing to use your products in the future.

Regards,

James Allan, MD

James Allan, MD
Family Physician

Keep the Dialogue Going

> "The trouble with her is that she lacks the power of conversation but not the power of speech."
>
> —George Bernard Shaw

Here are some final thoughts on your presentation. Average sales representatives look at their sales presentation as their turn to stand on the podium and preach. Too many sales presentations are one-sided and too "speech-like." Prospects, in general, are much more comfortable being involved in a conversation as opposed to being spoken to. So while you convey your solution, seek feedback and involvement from your customer. Your reward will be a selling environment that is much more conducive to open discussion which will more likely lead to a successful selling relationship.

> "A word is not a crystal, transparent and unchanged; it is the skin of a living thought, and may vary greatly in color and content according to the circumstances and the time in which it is used."
>
> —Oliver Wendell Holmes, opinion on *Towne v. Eisner*, January 7, 1918

If the "living thoughts" you have about your solution contain enthusiasm, excitement, and pride, then make sure the words you use to describe your product's benefits become the skin of those emotions. While PRECISE is about getting to the point, it is not about being boring while doing so. Say only what is necessary while making every one of your "conservatively used" words stir emotion. So don't just explain what your solution will do for them, show them how doing business with you will make their life better somehow…and do it with pure poetry.

Presentation Binders

I recommend that you carry a professional-looking binder that contains commonly used support materials. The goal here is to have all of your "stuff" in the same place so you become familiar with where it is. Being

PRECISE means never fumbling into a briefcase to look for something. Have all your important materials in one place at all times so you can easily get to it. I like mine to contain:

- Brochures
- Competitive information
- Financial information
- Promotion and special details
- Studies and white papers
- Testimonial letters

PRECISE Action #4
Review

- Convey Solution
- Load the bullets and shoot
- Do an individual presentation on each bullet
- Get agreement after each bullet
- Benefits, then features

Chapter Fifteen
PRECISE Action #5: Indecision— How to Conquer the Most Costly Barrier to the Top

> Main Entry: in·de·ci·sion
> Function: noun
> 1: reluctance or an inability to make up one's mind; irresolution
> 2: inability or unwillingness to decide
> 3: a wavering between two or more possible courses of action

Your ability to turn indecision into *decision* is an important action in PRECISE Selling. There are two parties that need to be decision-makers in any sales call. One is the salesperson and the other, the prospect. Too many salespeople look at sales as merely an exchange of information. While information sharing is necessary for decisions to be made that will benefit both parties, your objective should not be to deliver information. It should be to get a decision about your prospect's intentions in getting involved with your solution.

Prospects by nature often fear decision-making and their walls of defense are fortified with bricks of indecision. It is your job as the salesperson to break down those walls and knock their ass off the fence. But you must knock your ass off first.

A Posture of Imperturbability Can Ignite Decisions

> "In the first place, in the physician or surgeon no quality takes rank with imperturbability…imperturbability means coolness and presence of mind under all circumstances, calmness amid storm, clearness of judgment in moments of grave peril, immobility, and impassiveness.
>
> "It is the quality which is most appreciated by the laity though often misunderstood by them; and the physician who has them is fortunate to be without it, who betrays indecision and worry, and who shows that he is flustered and flurried in ordinary emergencies, loses rapidly the confidence of his patients."
>
> —Sir William Osler (1849–1919), Canadian-born British physician
> *In his Commencement Address at the*
> *University of Pennsylvania, May 1, 1889*

In sports, there are imperturbable names like John Elway, Mickey Mantle, and Michael Jordan that represent coolness under pressure. Well, doesn't pressure exist in your business? Isn't it what you feel when a customer doubts or expresses a concern about what you say or what you are selling? Be decisive and prospects will follow. Customers will respect, trust, and follow you if you act imperturbable. Even when your customer is perturbed, you must be the calm in the storm. This calmness will provide comfort and confidence and will produce a climate for action and decision.

George Patton had imperturbability. You need to also have it. The way you conduct yourself when a prospect has a doubt or concern has a direct impact on the outcome of the call. Your believability and credibility are tested every time a customer makes a statement like, "But the competition says…" You need to show imperturbability and coolness to help get your prospect over the hump. Get frazzled or defensive and your prospect will have a hard time overlooking it. Imperturbability is a quality of all top performers in any profession.

The paragraph above talks about the effects of a physician's coolness under pressure but can be easily translated to many other professions including sales.

When a customer has doubts or expresses indecision or concern, you should use that doubt as an opportunity to show the prospect how you handle pressure. How you respond to a concern is as important as what your response is. While the average sales rep becomes defensive and perturbed, it is the PRECISE sales rep that takes a breath, gets a gleam in her eye, and addresses those doubts. When it is done with confidence, calmness, and coolness, the importance of those doubts is often lessened.

You Asking for the Order

Have you ever walked out of a sales call clueless about what the prospect was thinking? Did they like what you said, or think you were full of crap? You think you might get the order, but you're just not sure? Of course you have. Unless you have a 100 percent close ratio it happens to all of us. What makes it so frustrating is that you often believe you did everything possible and for some reason the prospect just wouldn't budge. You might have received several minor agreements, a few buying signals, and even a confirmation from the prospect that they like and believe what you say. But as the call winds up, the prospect just politely smiles and asks you to leave some information, and that they will get back to you. This often occurs because the salesperson did not openly ask for a buying decision.

> "To decide not to decide is a decision. To fail to decide is a failure."
> —George S. Patton, Jr. (1885–1945), American army officer

There is an old saying in sales that says, "Ask for the order." While asking for the order is noble and necessary, a decision to ask for the order needs to be made first. So while selling to your prospects:

> *You* must make the decision to ask for a decision.

Unfortunately, many of us are afraid to do this. It drives us crazy that our prospect will not get off the fence, but we are often hypocrites when we let this bother us. We expect them to make a decision, even though we didn't ask them to make one.

What Causes Sales Rep Indecision?

In an earlier chapter we discussed the different types of sales representatives that exist. Those three types consisted of the Stereotypical Rep, Everybody's Friend, and the PRECISE Sales Rep. While there may be many pushy stereotypical salespeople out there, I believe there are many more that fall into the Everybody's Friend category. In my seminars I always ask my students to tell me if they feel they have a tendency to be either too pushy or not pushy enough. Usually nine out of ten students tell me that they wish they felt more comfortable when it came time to ask for the order.

Of the hundreds of sales courses that I have facilitated, I am yet to have one person tell me that their biggest sales challenge is that they "close too much." Not one has told me that they are constantly closing their prospects and have a tendency to make them angry because they're always forcing a decision. No, in fact, more of my students believe they have a tendency to just let a sale hang out there and float in the wind, hoping that all the pieces will just fall into place.

In the sales training world, there is a new politically correct, sensitive, and empathetic sales philosophy telling sales professionals that "old" closing techniques just don't work anymore. These books and seminars are teaching "how to master the art of indecision," and in the process, are teaching their students how to make the sales process longer and much more tedious than it needs to be.

The most efficient sales call is one where a decision about getting involved with your solution is made. That decision hopefully is a "yes" to your offering, but a "no" or a George Patton "we have decided not to decide," is fine, as long as some decision is made.

Indecision Wastes Time

Managing sales time is one of the more difficult tasks a salesperson faces. The PRECISE objective is to spend as little time as possible with as many customers as possible. This is a contradiction to the beliefs of most salespeople and sales managers. It is often difficult to distinguish between wasted time in front of a customer and valuable time. Salespeople waste countless hours making "follow-up" calls on previously visited or spoken to prospects. While follow-up calls are often necessary, they many times do little to advance the sale. But as salespeople, follow-up calls that include "face time" with the customer make us feel as if we are doing our job. They fill up our appointment schedule and fill our workday but often don't fill our bank account.

Indecision is often responsible for these many wasted follow-up calls. Making a decision to ask for a decision, during the first sales call (or first few depending on your sales cycle), can often save immeasurable hours, and this time can be spent prospecting for new business elsewhere.

Making a decision to ask for a decision needs to become a habit. Once it is, you will find that your prospects will be more honest with you. Salespeople are often apprehensive to ask for a decision because they're afraid of the potential answer. Don't worry about it! If they tell you no, find out the specific reasons they told you no and move on. Because the "no" they just gave you just saved you six personal follow-up calls, eight voice mail messages, and one ticked-off receptionist.

Sometimes customers can't decide how to let you down easy, so they string you along spewing misinformation while they are "killing you softly." Well, soft killings take too much time. Prying a decision from them as early as possible will allow you to move on to other opportunities. So encourage your prospects to make a decision and put you out of your misery as early as possible. It will mean money in your pocket down the road.

The Cost of a Delayed "No"

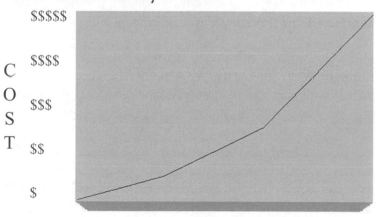

PRECISE Action #5   161

The Indianapolis 500 Sales Wreck

I once had a doctor prospect that had his office directly across the street from the Indianapolis Motor Speedway. He was an ear, nose, and throat physician who expressed some interest in our flexible, fiber-optic rhino-laryngoscope. (In case you're wondering, that's the skinny scope that looks like a black noodle that is inserted into the nose and down the throat to diagnose head and neck problems.) I did a demonstration for the doctor and impressed him with my nasal knowledge and anatomy. He drove that scope through the narrow turns of my nostrils like Mario Andretti cruising the speedway after throwing back a twelve-pack of Pabst Blue Ribbon.

What I mean is, he wasn't very good at the procedure, but at least he wore a smile as he tortured me. After shooting the breeze for about an hour, touching on everything from tonsils to carburetors, I thought the sale was in the bag. Toward the end of the call he told me he liked the scope and to leave some information. He then promised to get back to me by the end of the week. I believed what he said, smiled, and mentally put that sale in the books. At no time during that call did I ask him to make a decision about buying the scope. I felt like I had built a relationship in that short period of time and did not want to seem pushy and screw it up.

One week later I made a three-hour journey south from Chicago down to Indianapolis to follow up and hopefully pick up the order. I had called earlier in the week and was told the doctor would be in and would probably have a few moments to chat with me. When I got there, the receptionist said that he was too busy and would call me to reschedule. No problem— just a busy day. I will try again in a few days. About six unreturned phone calls and three more live "He's busy's," I was catching on.

> "Decision is a sharp knife that cuts clean and straight;
> indecision, a dull one that hacks and tears and leaves ragged edges behind it."
>
> —Gordon Graham

Well, this doctor finally dumped me. Sure enough, he had a deal with another manufacturer. And between me not asking for a decision during that first call, and his inability to tell me directly that he would not be buying my product, I wasted way too much time.

So ask for buying decisions, yea or nay, as early and as often as possible. And do it in a way that tells your prospects that your intent is not to push them into making a decision that they are not ready to make. And if after you ask, he is still wrapped in indecision, back off a bit, and make a note in your PDA or planner to follow up later. And don't torture them. While persistence can reap rewards, it can also be time-consuming. Go find five new prospects, convey your solution, and ask for a decision.

> This PRECISE activity will create more sales more often, and save you countless hours of wondering and wandering.

Indecision Land Mines

There are five reasons why prospects resist moving forward with an agreement or buying decision.

1. Lack of Information

PIC knowledge is important in preventing the indecision that can stall the momentum of a sales call. When a customer has a question that cannot be answered, this is often enough to prevent them from moving ahead. So prepare for every call, and never let "I am not sure" or "I'll get back to you" be responsible for a blown sale.

2. Lack of Emotion

One of the quotes that has stuck with me came from a well-known sales trainer named Tom Hopkins. He said, "People buy emotionally and defend it logically." If you want to turn that spark into a flame, throw some energy into your presentation. This will force your prospects to either enthusiastically say "yes" or enthusiastically say "no." And remember, who cares? At least it is a decision.

3. Lack of Credibility

Prospects need to believe that what you are saying is true. They may love your product or service, but if you have not earned their respect and trust, it is difficult to get them to make a decision. Remember, the first products that you need to sell are yourself and your company. After doing that, make sure they know that your objective is to find out what their needs and wants are, and then find the PRECISE solution to fill those needs and wants. If your solution is not right for the prospect, then don't sell it. You know the old saying; "She was such a good salesperson that she could sell ice to the Eskimos." While she might have gotten the order, I guarantee you those Eskimos were piping hot once they realized they were duped.

4. Lack of Urgency

Urgency is an important ingredient in stirring sales activity. Without it, prospects will rarely buy your solution. As discussed in an earlier chapter, a prospect must understand the need for a solution like yours before they understand details of your specific solution. There are two types of needs. There are *observable needs* and *hidden needs*. Observable needs often carry urgency; hidden needs do not. Observable needs are often openly stated and made clear to the salesperson. Hidden needs, on the other hand, are not obvious to either the prospect or the salesperson. When an observable need exists, prospects most often know a change or new investment needs to be made. So the salesperson need not waste time convincing them of this.

When a prospect already sees a need, the salesperson's only job is to convince them that it is their product and not the competition's that can fulfill those needs. Hidden needs, on the other hand, must be transformed into observable needs if the salesperson is to be successful. So remember…before you sell your product, use questions to see if an observable need either exists or needs to be created.

5. Doubts and Concerns

Doubts, concerns, and objections can and often do exist in successful selling. They often feel like speed bumps in the sale, but if you handle them correctly, you can use them to create urgency.

Doubts and concerns are not a bad thing. They tell you the prospect's mind is cooking a little. And when the mind is cooking, you can often smell the emotions. When prospects share a concern or doubt, they are often posing a challenge. A challenge is an open door to prove yourself. When there is little response either way, and the customer simply tells you to leave some information, aren't you worse off than if she told you exactly why she was stalling you? PRECISE Selling is about open communication. You either have the solution that will work, or you don't. If your prospect has a concern, you always want to know about it.

Address Decision-Making Concerns with Precision

The two ways to PRECISE-ly reduce the impact of concerns and doubts:

1. Help your prospect minimize the importance of those concerns by making all the benefits of your solution so much larger.
2. Address what is causing the concern head on; but only after you are sure you know exactly what the real concern is.

Lessen the Importance of Specific Concerns

I want you to pretend that you are bringing a scale into every sales call. On one side of the scale are all the benefits that your solution can provide. On the other side are all the doubts and concerns that your prospect has about your solution. At the end of your call, the scale must be clearly tipped toward the benefit side. This is not to say the doubt and concern side needs to be empty, it just needs to weigh less than the benefit side.

Benefits vs. Concerns Scale

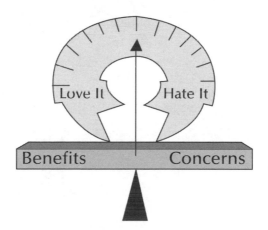

If you have already gone through PRECISE Actions #1 through #4, and have focused your solution presentation on the bullets they expressed and their benefits, chances are that you have done a pretty good job loading up the benefit side of this equation. This is why it is so important to separate each bullet into its own presentation and get individual "little yeses" during the Convey Solution Action. Each "little yes" becomes a weight on the scale and tips the sale toward the "love it" side. It's helpful to load up the benefit side of the scale before doubt or concern enters the equation. Once the scale is tipping in one direction, its momentum makes it difficult to get the needle moving in the other direction. Once you have that scale working for you, it's okay to have a few weights put on the other side—because your PRECISE benefits weigh a hell of a lot more.

Uh Oh…My Competition Really Is Better

There will be times when your solution may be inferior to your competition in specific areas. That too is okay. If you know this is the case, then give that weight to your prospects. Let them put it on the "concerns" side of your scale. Do not fight them on it. Help them realize that all the benefits that your product or service can provide will outweigh the few concerns or doubts that they may have. Minimize their importance by maximizing your bullets and benefits.

In the next chapter we will discuss how to address customer concerns and doubts head-on.

Chapter Sixteen

Damn, You Are a SHARP Addresser: Five Steps to Help You Respond to "Indecision-Causing" Concerns

Main Entry: 1sharp
Function: adjective
1: keen in intellect
2: having or showing alert competence and clear understanding
3: capable of acting or reacting strongly
4: implies quick perception, clever resourcefulness, or sometimes questionable trickiness

Be SHARP When Addressing Concerns

Prospects will throw objections and concerns at you. When this happens, you need to address them head on. To do this, you need to be SHARP. Let's discuss what it means to be SHARP by looking at each of the four definitions above.

SHARP Intellect

> "What is the hardest task in the world? To think."
> —Ralph Waldo Emerson (1803–1882),
> American essayist, poet, and philosopher

Don't get rattled when a prospect has an area of concern. Pause for a moment, use that intellect of yours, and get to the bottom of it. Once you know exactly what the prospect's concern is, just tap into that vault of knowledge that you worked so hard to acquire.

Now I wouldn't exactly call myself intellectual, but before I walk in the door to sell my solution, I make sure I have sufficiently stuffed my head with as much PIC knowledge as it can handle. When your prospects fire an "indecision" causing concern or objection, you must be prepared to respond with something that puts their mind at ease and advances the sale. This is where plenty of PIC (Product, Industry, Competition) knowledge is crucial. It is difficult to sound SHARP and intellectual when you cannot answer a question or concern.

SHARP Competence

Showing alert competence means having the ability to provide a solution to problems. As we discussed in an earlier chapter, alert eyes and ears are crucial during a sales call. If you are not closely watching and alertly listening to your prospect, then you might miss something they are trying to tell you. Unfortunately, prospects are sometimes ambiguous when voicing doubts or concerns. Sometimes they mean to be unclear, and sometimes they just have trouble putting into words exactly what their concern is. Either way, it is important that you are alertly competent, so you can effectively address those concerns that stand in the way of you carrying out your objective. When you are alert, and when you know your stuff, it will be difficult for your customer to intentionally or unintentionally sneak anything by you.

> "Trying to sneak a pitch past Hank Aaron is like trying to sneak the sunrise past a rooster."
>
> —Joe Adcock, Milwaukee Braves first baseman

SHARP and Clear Understanding

To effectively address an area of concern, you must first understand exactly what that concern is. Many salespeople take time addressing the wrong area of concern because they lack a clear understanding of what is troubling their prospect. Customers often say one thing but mean another. The only way to clearly understand what is in your prospect's heart and head is to question them. By doing this, you'll be able to identify what specific issue needs to be addressed.

SHARP Capability to Act or React Strongly

How quickly do you react when a customer throws you an objection or a concern? Your ability to quickly respond could mean the difference between you getting the order or going home empty-handed. As mentioned in an earlier chapter, sales is a lot like fishing. While fishing can be rewarding and profitable, the story below will demonstrate the importance of making quick decisions.

Bill was the best fisherman on Skaneateles Lake. While the other fishing enthusiasts from the village would be lucky to pull in one or two fish a day, Bill would come back from his "secret fishing spot" soaking wet and with buckets full of bass and lake trout. Bill was the talk of the town. Dave, the local game warden, began to catch on to this and grew curious and a bit concerned. He approached Bill and asked him if he could join him on his next outing.

After walking about a mile and a half through a dense trail, they arrived at their destination. Bill then reached into a backpack he carried and pulled out a small round object. As Dave looked more closely, he noticed it was a hand grenade. Bill removed the pin, and then tossed it underhand out into the water as if he was tossing a horseshoe at a stake. They were soaked. Seconds later, dozens of the best looking bass and lake trout you have ever seen began floating to the surface. Bill let out a "yahoo," grabbed his net and entered the water, scooping up one fish after another.

Immediately, Dave lost his mind, telling Bill that he would never fish on Skaneateles Lake as long as he lived. Dave wrote up a summons and handed it to Bill as he threw his "trophies" into a large bucket. Bill then reached into his backpack, pulled out another grenade, pulled the pin, and handed it to Dave. Dave froze for a moment as Bill said, "Hello, it's fishin' time. Are you with me?" Dave had to make a quick decision. In two quick seconds, he went from spectator to participant. A big-time decision had to be made, and made fast!

A sales call is often just like that. Everything is going smoothly until your prospect throws you a grenade, and you are forced to react and make a decision quickly. Delay or "lock up," and you are "dead." React quickly and decisively and you will not only survive this sales call, but live to participate in several more.

Velvet Conviction

Doubts and concerns often arise quickly and out of nowhere, and you should prepare to overcome them with "velvet conviction." "Velvet conviction" is a strong, decisive response, delivered in a yielding way. It is attacking the doubts and concerns quickly without attacking your prospect. For instance, let's say you're in the middle of your presentation and a customer blurts out, "Your competition was in here yesterday and says that your quality is horrible." If you're like me, every cell in your body tells you that you should curl up your top lip and call the lying idiot a…well…*lying idiot*! Unfortunately, this would probably blow it for us. So what do we do? Try taking a deep breath, count to three, and then say "lying idiot!" Wait a minute. See, I told you it's hard. I mean…take that breath, count to three and use your questioning skills to get to the bottom of your prospect's concerns. Remember, the goal is to get the customer to be as open and honest with us a they possibly can. Because in that honesty is the key to the sale. If we act negatively or defensive, they will be too uncomfortable to be honest. We want the truth, and nothing but the truth and should appreciate when they give it to us, even if we don't like what we hear.

SHARP, Quick Perception

Addressing areas of concern can be lots of fun. It is the most challenging part of a sales presentation, and it is in this ability that top sales performers separate themselves from the average. Notice how Abe Lincoln combines quick perception and questioning techniques to help his "prospect" understand his reasoning.

Failing to convince an opponent that his reasoning was faulty, Abraham Lincoln asked him, "Well, tell me how many legs has a cow?"

"Four, of course," was the quick reply.

"That's right," said Lincoln. "Now suppose we call the cow's tail a leg, how many legs would the cow have?"

"Why, five, obviously."

"That's where you are wrong," replied Lincoln. "Simply calling a cow's tail a leg doesn't make it a leg."

PRECISE sales reps have the ability to use leading questions, rather than statements, to make prospects see things in a different way.

SHARP, Clever Resourcefulness

> "A series of great opportunities, brilliantly disguised as insoluble problems."
>
> —John W. Gardner (1912–2002),
> former U.S. Secretary of Health, Education, and Welfare

Being resourceful means finding answers and solutions where none exist. This does not mean telling half-truths or misleading customers. It does mean thinking creatively to overcome an area of concern.

One of the most clever and resourceful solutions I have heard came from an inspection service company that sells long flexible scopes (some over a hundred feet) as well as small, motorized, robotic cameras to inspect pipes, channels, and deep, dark canals of all types, shapes and sizes. Their market is mostly fossil fuel, nuclear, and chemical plants.

This company had a client with what you might call a "special need," and some big problems. There was some debris that had been clogging a large pipe that was critical to plant operation. This debris needed to be removed or the plant would have to shut down, costing hundreds of thousands of dollars.

The inspection company sales rep took the dimensions of the pipe and determined that his scope could effectively pass through it. The real challenge, however, was the large size of the clogging debris, as he had no acceptable way of removing it once his scope found it. The only solution seemed to be to burrow into the side of the large, concrete pipe wall, and that would take a total plant shut down, once again, costing several hundred thousand dollars.

After cooking his clever and resourceful mind for a bit, the sales rep had a "leap of consciousness." After some detailed questioning of the client, the sales rep determined that they needed to physically get somebody into that pipe to remove the debris. The reality was, the channel was too small for the average-size adult. That's when it hit this clever fellow.

"Too big for an average-size adult. What about a not-so-average-size adult?"

Two days later he arrived with a dwarf who himself proved to be quite resourceful. This gentleman was small enough to fit into the pipe and large enough to perform the necessary task. He slid his way down the pipe and quickly removed the debris. And after scurrying his way back out of the pipe, he was then able to give a detailed account of the condition of the pipe and of any other damage that might have occurred. In the end, hundreds of thousands of dollars were saved, and the inspection service company made a client for life. My friend, that is SHARP and clever resourcefulness. And believe me, this was no small task.

The Five SHARP Steps to Addressing an Area of Concern

Remember, the goal is to do things well repeatably. That includes answering the indecision-causing barriers to the sale in a precise and organized way. Train your mind to act this way every time you hear an objection, and you will be able to put your customers mind at ease.

1. **S**top
2. **H**ear
3. **A**sk
4. **R**espond
5. **P**ack it with agreement

1. Stop

"Sometimes it is very urgent to wait." ("Es muy importante esperar.")
—General Francisco Franco (1892–1975),
Spanish soldier and dictator

When a prospect has a concern, it is urgent. So wait! Do not sound defensive. Do not snap back. This is one of the most difficult yet most important tasks a salesperson has to perform. Unfortunately, patience is not always our profession's best virtue. So the next time a prospect delivers a concern, doubt, or objection, *stop*, wait…count to three…and move to Step #2.

2. Hear

While stopping yourself from jumping all over an area of concern does take some energy, it takes even more effort to focus and *hear* exactly what your customer is trying to tell you. As mentioned earlier, some prospects have no problem explaining the specifics that caused their doubts. Others might throw you a small clue, which is often a small "stall," hoping that you will not get to the bottom of what they are thinking and feeling. But if you have the ability to get beyond words by clearly hearing and understanding the specifics and the importance of those words, you will then be able to effectively get around them. When you are not completely sure of the specific area of concern, or are curious about the importance of it, move to SHARP Step #3.

3. Ask a Question

It is important that you address the specific concerns that are causing indecision. To do this, simply ask questions. And ask questions until you are sure you know what your prospect is thinking and feeling. Only then should you deliver a response to the customer's concern. Too many salespeople neglect this step because they feel that they already know what the prospect is thinking. Don't do this. Don't assume. Let me give you a real-life example of why it is important to not assume you know what's in the customer's head.

I used to sell a product known as a video colposcope. This device is essentially a highly magnified video camera on a mobile stand that is used to perform female cervical examinations. These exams are traditionally performed with an optical system that closely resembles a microscope. So when my company developed a system that would now project a video image of the cervix onto a video monitor, it was looked at with some skepticism. Clarity of image is crucial during this exam, as the physician needs to be able to detect subtle changes in the cervical tissue.

One day I made a sales call on a large OB/GYN practice in Chicago. They had seen the video colposcope at a convention, and wanted a salesperson to come by for further discussion and a demonstration. Things were going great as I performed the first four PRECISE Actions of Prepare, Respect and Trust, Engage with Questions, and Convey Solution. It was then that one physician threw me a concern.

He said, "I am concerned that I will not get a three-dimensional image when looking at the cervix on a video monitor, as I do with my optical scope."

Thinking that I knew exactly what he meant, I continued to address what I thought was his concern without ever *stopping, hearing,* and *asking*.

I quickly and assumptively answered with, "Doctor, I can understand your concern. But many OB/GYNs that are now using our system have found the clarity on the video monitor is sufficient enough to notice any subtle tissue changes."

He responded with, "Oh." (He really meant "Oh, crap!"). He continued with, "I was more concerned about getting a three-dimensional image for when I take biopsies. I'm afraid that I will misjudge how much tissue I need to take. But now that you mention visualization of the tissue, I guess that is a concern as well."

I blew it! By neglecting the S, H, and A steps, I addressed the wrong concern and in doing so, I created a new one. So now he had one of his own and one that I nicely created and handed to him. Nice job, Sullivan.

This is how I should have handled the concern.

Prospect: "I am concerned that I will not get a three-dimensional image when looking at the cervix on a video monitor as I do with my optical scope."

Sullivan *stops*, shuts up, and *hears* everything the prospect is trying to say. Because the concern that he *hears* is not specific enough, he goes on to *ask*:

Sullivan: "Doctor, can you please help me better understand how you think not having a three-dimensional image will affect your procedure?"

Prospect: "I'm afraid that I will misjudge how much tissue I need to take from the cervix."

Bingo! Okay, now I have enough to go on. I will make sure my response helps him understand how my system can, in fact, make it easier for him to perform biopsies. I will stay focused in this area and be careful not to bring up any other areas of concern.

I hope this helps you learn from my lesson. Even when you think that you know what the customer means, *ask* him for clarification. This will prevent you from creating another concern and ensure that you address the real one.

⊙ 4. Respond

Only after you have completed the S, H, and A, is it safe to respond. Make your response PRECISE by using limited dialogue to address the specific concern that you were able to identify. Tell them that you understand their concerns, and do not lessen the importance of their opinion by saying, "I have never heard that one before." Be prepared to dig into that presentation binder that you assembled and pull out any studies or testimonial letters that will help you back up your response. Treat this response like a bullet and deliver a focused presentation only on that concern. Do not go off on a tangent in another direction.

If you know your product, industry, and competition well, you no doubt have an idea about some of the objections and concerns that you might hear more than others. For instance, if you know that your product's price is 20 percent higher than your competition, you need to be prepared with a smooth and confident response about why its performance justifies the higher cost. If your company is new to the industry and has no track record, you should prepare a response that will confidently convince your prospect there is little risk in working with you.

These are just two examples, but I am sure there are many more common concerns that you may hear from potential customers on any given day. In the space below, I would like you to list the five concerns that you hear most about your solution. If you sell several different products or services, do this exercise for each one on a separate sheet of paper.

1. _____

2. _____

3. _____

4. _____

5. _____

Let me show you an example for one of my products.

1. I have concerns about the accuracy of your system.

2. Your competition offers a more comprehensive solution.

3. Your product costs more than theirs.

4. You use a different technology than the market leader.

5. Your product is bigger and bulkier than the competition.

Now, on a separate sheet of paper, I would like you to develop a response to each one of your commonly heard concerns that you listed. Take time to think about the perfect response and draw it up as if you were Steven Spielberg developing a script for an Academy Award-winning movie. I then want you to transform yourself from Steven Spielberg into your favorite actor. Rehearse your response as if you are preparing for a "shoot" that will someday end up on the silver screen. I am not kidding when I say this! Develop the perfect response, write it down, rehearse it, and get "fired up" when you actually have a chance to use it. Think of how prepared and powerful you will feel the next time you hear your commonly heard concern flow from the lips of your customer. You will be ready to confidently and SHARP-ly address it head-on—and sound smooth as hell while doing so.

I have done this for several years now and it has meant tens of thousands of dollars to me. I almost look forward to hearing a concern that I am prepared for, because it gives me a chance to put to use the lines that I practiced.

Now, I know you might be saying, "I hate canned responses…because they sound so…canned." Well, guess what? They only sound canned when they are not practiced and rehearsed well and often enough. There are differences between soap opera actors and Academy Award winners, and those differences are ability and practice. I know you have the ability, so now it just takes practice. Do this exercise and you will increase your sales by at least 20 percent this year.

◎ 5. Pack it Up with Agreement

When you are done with your "Silver Screen" response, you need to get confirmation and agreement that you have sufficiently addressed the prospects' concerns. If you have not answered their concerns enough, then try again until you do. And when you finally convince them that your solution will do the job, get confirmation that you convinced them. If not, at least get confirmation that you did not convince them, and then move on. Remember, in the end, it is acceptable to agree to disagree. If they "make a decision to not make a decision" on your solution, at least you will know exactly why that is. This will save you much wondering, worrying, and wasted time.

And if you and your prospect agree on your response, move away from that concern as quickly as possible with a Detail Question. Detail Questions are effective at taking your customer's mind away from their previous concern and on to a new topic. I will usually ask a question that has to do with the physical use of my product. An example would be, "Doctor, I am glad you are confident that with practice, you can become proficient at performing biopsies with the video scope. Now I am curious. In which room will you be performing the procedures?"

I learn a lot from a prospect's response to a Detail Question such as this. If they began to tell me specifics like which room, I have a pretty good idea the benefits side of the sales scale is tipping in my direction.

After you have answered your prospect's concerns and the sales call is flowing exactly as you had planned, it's time to Secure and Advance (PRECISE Action #6). This is where the PRECISE sales rep really has fun.

PRECISE Action
#5 Review

Indecision—Overcome Theirs and Yours
"Make a decision to ask for a decision."
1. **S**top
2. **H**ear
3. **A**sk
4. **R**espond
5. **P**ack it with agreement

Chapter Seventeen
PRECISE Action #6: Secure Agreement and Advance— Take 'em to the Promised Land

Main Entry: 'secure
Function: verb
1: to put beyond hazard of losing or of not receiving
Main Entry: 'advance
Function: noun
1: a moving forward
2: progress in development

"Yes." "Hmmm." "That's nice." "Wow." "Okay." "How much?" These are what we call security alarms. These are the indicators that the customer is ready to buy. It is time to curb your insatiable appetite to say just a little more with hopes of getting your customer even more excited than they already are. I have seen some fine sales reps enter a presentation as if they were entering a boxing ring. They feel once they have a customer on the ropes, they really need to knock 'em out with a few more feature jabs and benefit hooks. Well, guess what? We aren't boxing, so we need to chill out and be PRECISE.

Know When to Say When
A key fundamental in PRECISE Selling is saying only words that will advance the sale and no more. It means knowing not to use a bunker buster bomb when all it will take is a rocket-propelled grenade. The reason we use only enough is because our ability to say less will help us say more.

Think about it. When somebody is selling to you and pounds you with too much information, do you have a tendency to shut down? And when this happens, isn't it difficult to remember what the salesperson even said? But when they give you just enough to educate and excite you (and no more), aren't you more satisfied. It's like eating a bag of candy. In fact, as the following story shows, it's exactly like that.

Christmas in Connecticut was delightful at age eight, as an extended family consisting of over thirty-five cousins would gather to celebrate. The year was 1976 and the Christmas Day party was hopping. As a large Irish Catholic family, the parents had no problem throwing back a little booze to celebrate the festive occasion. Well, at age eight, I was a little too young to dabble in the Guinness, but I knew my time would come. Meanwhile, Butterfingers were my vice. I could not get enough of them…so I thought.

So at two o'clock on Christmas Day in 1976, my cousin Matt and I made our trek through six backyards, over two fences, through three alleys, and wound up at Cavanaugh's Convenience Store. I made my way straight to the Butterfingers. At first I just grabbed one, then realizing it was Christmas, I changed my mind. "Mr. Cav, give me a whole bag of bite-size Butterfingers," I said.

Well, he did. After that first bite, I was in pure ecstasy and the smell of Christmas in the air made my Butterfinger that much better. As I took my second bite, I looked at my full bag of candy with conviction, fully aware of the daunting task ahead of me. As I wrapped my chocolate-smeared, chapped lips around the second Butterfinger, time stood still. Could number two actually be better than number one? *Yes*. And never mind number three. Maybe my taste buds were sleeping during the first two, because this 'finger was awe-inspiring. I could hardly wait for number four, five, six, and seven. Well, two bites into number seven, something strange began to happen. My stomach began to reject Butterfinger number seven like a human body rejects a donor organ. Fight through it, Sullivan! You can do it!

Now Butterfingers are some tasty candy bars. They're all crunchy, peanut-buttery, and chocolaty, and they go great on ice cream. But scientific research shows there is a law of diminishing returns as it relates to the Butterfinger. Please observe figure (A).

Figure (A)

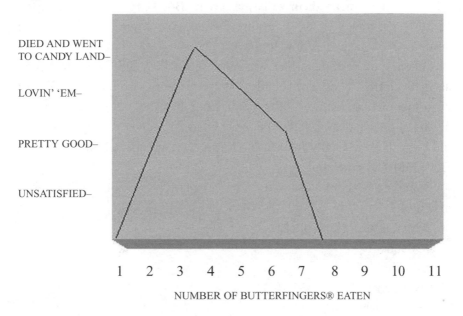

DIED AND WENT
TO CANDY LAND–

LOVIN' 'EM–

PRETTY GOOD–

UNSATISFIED–

1 2 3 4 5 6 7 8 9 10 11

NUMBER OF BUTTERFINGERS® EATEN

After old number seven, my teeth had turned completely black, and I looked like I had camouflaged my face with milk chocolate. As I took my second bite, my stomach locked up and it felt as if somebody had put a car jack underneath the back of my tongue. What was happening? Well, it seemed the family of seven Butterfingers would have rather spent Christmas Day on the concrete surface of Fern Street than in the warm cozy confines of my stomach (in short, I threw up).

Since that day, these chapped lips have never touched another Butterfinger. I learned my lesson that too much of a good thing can be really bad. Had I only stopped after number three, I would still be eating Butterfingers today. And think of all the enjoyment I have missed without the extra twenty-five pounds. What a shame!

Precise Sales Reps Don't Let Their Prospects Get Sick

When presenting your solution, look at your bullets as Butterfingers. Give your prospects only what they need and no more. Leave them in pure ecstasy and longing for more. Make them so excited about those three Butterfingers that they can't wait to sink their teeth into them. Don't make the mistake of the average sales rep that keeps feeding the prospect with

Butterfingers until they get to number seven and make them sick. If it takes seven to make them satisfied, great. But keep asking after each Butterfinger how your prospects are feeling. And when they get that big smile on their face, it is time to move.

When your customers like what they hear, they will begin to sound security alarms. These are sounds that are projected from any number of customer orifices but most often come from the mouth or throat…but not always. I once had a customer get so excited throughout the upper half of his body, that he totally relaxed his lower half; specifically his buttocks. Boy, did I feel powerful!

Some more common—and more hygienic—examples of security alarms are:

"Hmmmmm." (high pitch)

"Oooooooo."

"Ahhhhhhh."

"Woooooow."

"How much?"

They are usually combined with some hand or body gesture that tells you that your solution presentation is working. When you hear and see these signals, it's time to close up the bag and move forward.

Secure Solution Agreement

After the security alarms go off, get confirmation from your prospects that you are reading them correctly. Keep it simple by asking a simple security question like:

> "So, can you see how my solution will make your life easier by _____?"

In the _____, fill in some of the bullet benefits that you discussed and ones they already agreed with in the Convey Solution Action. This is a short way of recapping, wrapping up tightly, and securing the prospect's emotions. It is like taking a PRECISE sales calculator and adding:

Little Yes + Little Yes + Little Yes + Little Yes + Security Alarm + Security Question=*One Big Fat Yes*

This equation only works when you combine Little Yeses, a Security Alarm, and a Security Question. Don't expect to press that equals sign on your sales calculator and get the Big Yes if you didn't add in the necessary factors.

Show Them the Money

Prospects will not sign up for your solution until they know how much it will cost them. Try to separate your product discussion from the financial discussion when possible. Many times it makes no sense to even discuss the "how much" until you feel confident that you have established:

- They have an observable need
- Your product provides a solution
- They should have a sense of urgency

Once you have fulfilled these three, it's time to talk money. The transition between solution discussion and financial discussion is often uncomfortable for both sales rep and prospect. Sales reps love talking about their product or service, but often clam up and appear apologetic at this point in a sale. Don't apologize. Don't even appear apologetic about having to tell them how much your solution costs. Put a smile on your face and act as if the greatest part of your discussion is about to unfold. This sets a positive tone to an otherwise uncomfortable experience. It is important that your prospects' walls do not come up. You can prevent this by keeping the tempo of your presentation steady and positive.

An Effective Transition

If I haven't hammered you enough about the effectiveness of repeatability, let me take another shot at it. You know that you will talk about the finances of your solution on almost every call you make, with some exceptions. Which means you know that you will make a transition from your product or service presentation into a discussion about cost. So, it is helpful to have a prepared and rehearsed transition statement that smoothly moves you out of the product or service discussion and into the money.

This is one that I use every time:

"Let's see if it makes financial sense."

I love these seven words because they smoothly get you into your financial discussion without putting stress on your prospect. In fact, by using the words, "Let's see . . ." you will reduce pressure because you are not telling your prospect the cost will make sense. On the contrary, you are telling them that you will provide the needed information for them to make their own financial decision…with a little help from you, of course.

Know the Money Like You Know Your Product

Treat your financial discussion like a product itself. Your prospect can love every feature and benefit that your product or company can provide, but unless you convince them the cost justifies the benefits, you will not get a sale.

I have seen too many fine salespeople do a fantastic job of convincing their prospects of the benefits of their solution only to completely blow it during the financial discussion. If you sell products or services that cost tens of thousands of dollars, then you may be presenting several different financing options. With these different options often comes different paperwork that needs to be authorized by the prospect. Never enter a sales call without all the necessary financial paperwork. This can destroy the flow of the call and prevent you from getting the order. Bring all of it with you.

It is not only important to bring your order forms, leasing agreements, sign up sheets, or whatever you may call them. It is also crucial that you become intimately familiar with every word on those sheets. Know every detail (and where every bit of customer information needs to go) as well as you know every detail of your product itself. I cannot stress this enough. I have seen too many sales lost because the sales rep did not feel comfortable with the tools necessary to close the sale. As a result, indecision sets in for both sales rep and prospect and often leads to the dreaded, "Let me get some paperwork together, and I will get back to you." Ugh! I can hardly stand to write those words. The sales reps that make this sentence part of their everyday selling vocabulary might as well just say:

"I am unprepared to close the sale today and pray to God above that you will still be interested when I fax over the information. And I hope you understand the contract because I sure as hell don't. You see…I'm a product guy. I leave the finances to someone else."

Being PRECISE is about providing a solution. It is impossible to do this without a comprehensive knowledge of the financial options that are available for them. In the end, the benefits of your solution must justify the cost. That's it! So if you only perform well at presenting your solution benefits and perform poorly at the cost discussion, you only get a 50 percent on the "sales test." Where I come from, that's an "F."

Advancing the Sale

Watch your prospect's behavior and listen closely to how they respond to your financial package. If they give you Positive Financial Security Alarms, it is time to *advance* the sale. Positive body language and security alarms should be enough of a green light for you to try to gain commitment. So don't feel the need to ask if the finances make sense if the alarms already told you that they do. Remember, being PRECISE means saying as little as possible to carry out your objective.

At this point, use what is commonly known as an "assumptive close." This is time where the PRECISE Sales Rep puts all indecision aside, takes control, and leaves no sale dangling in the wind. While the average salesperson locks up, the PRECISE Performer is moving forward.

> "He who moves not forward, goes backward."
> —Johann Wolfgang von Goethe (1749–1832),
> German author and poet

To *advance* the sale out of the presentation phase and into the post sale phase try a "Detail/Two-Choice" Question. An example would be:

> "Great, John. I'm glad the finances make sense. Then with your permission, I would like to get a date scheduled in my planner when it would be most convenient for your staff to become trained on the use of our system. Would next week or the following week work better for your people?"

Let's break it down:

"With your permission."

These words are very important in helping you to keep the customer feeling pressure free. They must always feel as if they are in control, and these three words help you do this.

"...date scheduled"

This is advancing at its finest. It is an attempt to turn your presentation into a concrete order. Much security comes from getting you or your company's name into their scheduling book for a follow-up, post sale visit. In the case where it is a multi-call sale, and where your objective is not to get an order but instead to get a commitment to take the decision to the next level, these words are equally effective. It takes commitment on your customers' part to schedule a time to see you again. They only do this when they feel secure.

(If your solution does not require a follow-up visit or an installation, then feel free to ignore the last paragraph.)

"...become trained..."

These words take your prospect mentally away from "considering your solution," to mentally "using your solution." When their mind begins using your product, the rest of their body is not far behind. These are two more words that are effective in advancing your sale. While my example uses post-sale training in an attempt to take the customer's mind out of the sale and into the post-sale future, there are many ways you can accomplish the same goal. The words "become trained" can be easily replaced with things like "install the system," "review your inventory," "run the reports," whatever. The words you use just need to include an action that your customer would do "assuming" they decided to move forward. And when I say moving forward, I don't necessarily mean signing your order form or giving you the final approval. For many of us, selling is a multiple stage process. You can use this same technique to get to the next stage of the sale. Either way, get them emotionally involved in the post-sale use of your solution, and watch their reaction. If they begin to answer your questions, it's a good indication that they are moving in the right direction.

"Would next week or the following week . . ."

This is your classic Detail/Two-Choice Question. If your customer is accepting of your advance, they will answer your question with one of the two choices that you presented. Or neither one of your choices might make sense for him, so instead he provides a third choice. Who cares! You love them all! They all mean the sale is advancing.

Make a habit of reacting to financial security alarms in this way. When your mind is trained to advance at the first sound of the alarm, it will do so on every sale. There will be no indecision, no floundering, and no "Do you have any more questions?" When the alarms go off, they sound a lot like this:

"I love it, I want it, and the benefits justify the cost. So don't ask me if I have any more questions, and don't ask me if I want to buy it. Just trust what my alarms are telling you and move it, sister!"

Secure Financial Agreement When No Alarms Are Sounding

Sometimes after discussing finances, you hear no alarms. Perhaps your package was more than they expected, or perhaps they just prefer to hold their reactions close to the vest. At this point, use some of the PRECISE Questioning techniques that we discussed to try to get some reaction from your prospect.

Try something like, "Can you see how _____ (fill in your *benefits*) might be worth the investment?" Or "What are your thoughts on the investment amount?"

Remember, you don't care if they love the price or hate it. You just need to make sure that you know where they stand. If they give you a positive reaction, then advance them with a Detail/Two-Choice Question. If they tell you that it is more than they expected, then find out "how much more" and then revisit the bullets that you discussed earlier with hopes of adding more value into them. Remember, the benefits must justify the cost.

So if the cost is weighing more than the benefits, than something has to give. Either the benefits need to weigh more, or your cost needs to weigh less. PRECISE salespeople prefer to pump up the benefits long before adjusting cost. You know the old saying, "You're customer is number one." It's crap! Your family is number one. Keep your margin up and buy a family member something nice with the extra dough.

Discounting is taking the easy way out!

And if you have to give up a little something, make your customer feel as if it is the most painful thing you have ever done. And never give without getting; otherwise your gifts will have no worth.

Advancing the Sale Up the Decision-Making Chain

As mentioned earlier, the business world today is more complicated than ever. Corporate bureaucracies are fatter, and it seems everybody has their hand in the decision-making process. Despite this, it is still crucial that you Secure and Advance every step along the way. Your objective should be to get agreement from your current audience whether they are the final decision maker or just an "influencer." Just as a bunch of Little Yeses in a sale equal one Big Yes, a bunch of Little Yeses at each step in the decision-making chain will also lead to one Big Yes. So don't assume that it is enough simply to provide information at each decision-making step. In fact, in most cases, all seven PRECISE Actions can be performed with every decision maker at every step in the decision-making chain of command.

The Gates Are Closed

Sometimes you have gone up the chain as far as you can go. You ask to meet with a higher-level decision maker, and you are met with resistance. In many industries this happens all the time. When it does, your objective needs to be:

Get agreement from your current prospect and influencer that they believe in your solution.

Make Them Semi-PRECISE

First things first. You first have to convince your lower level, limited decision-making prospect that yours is a solution worth representing. These lower-level decision-makers people are often buyers, purchasing agents and materials managers. They can also be users of the product and not necessarily the people that hold the purse strings. Regardless, you need to hear from them that their life would be better off with you and your solution in it. Once you do, it is time to make them PRECISE. (I recommend you get online, buy a copy of *20 Days to the Top* and hand it to them. And while you are there, go ahead and pick yourself up a couple of extra copies.)

I am obviously kidding about the book-buying thing, but I am not kidding about turning them into a salesperson. If you will not be able to deliver your presentation to the people that make the decisions, then you have no choice but to help them become better at delivering your message.

Step #1

If they *did* control the money, would your solution be the one that they would invest in? To find out, ask them:

You: "Bill, would you be happy if your company switched to our product?"

Once you get a yes, move to Step #2.

Step #2

Ask them to tell you what message will resonate most with the key decision-makers. An example:

You: "Bill, I know you like our product's ability to save you tons of time and make your workday easier. But what do you think is most important to the key decision-makers as it relates to making a possible change?"

Bill: "Well, I think they will love the fact that they will save thousands of dollars each year by making the change."

You: "Anything else?"

Bill: "Well, I'm sure they'll like that the product will make the staff's job much easier. Morale has been a little low around here, and this would show an investment in our people's happiness."

This is where you can help a bit. If Bill missed a key benefit that you think the key decision-makers would value, then make him aware of it.

You: "And do you think they will recognize that our product will make for a safer work environment, which just might keep the company's insurance rates down?"

Bill: "Yes, I forgot about that. They are always trying to improve work conditions."

Notice what you did here. You just had a nice little dress rehearsal, and turned this guy into a semi-PRECISE selling machine.

Always Remember Your Objective

Never forget why you are there, and keep working toward that goal during the call. Remove all indecision and fear, and leave no loose ends. If you consistently Secure Agreement and Advance your sale, you will rarely walk out of a sales call saying, "I have no idea what they are thinking." You will have either met your goal or you have not. And you will know if you have because you "made a decision to ask for a decision."

Remember that "no" and "I don't think it is going to work," are responses almost as good as "I'll take it," and ones that will save you many wasted hours and the dollars that go with them. Encourage your customer to tell you exactly how they feel, and make it easy for them to do so by keeping a positive attitude.

PRECISE Action
 # 6 Review

- Secure Agreement and Advance
- Confirm that they like your solution
- Confirm benefits justify Cost
- Advance with "Detail/Two-Choice" Question
- Multiple decision-makers—make your last contact semi-PRECISE

PRECISE Action #7: Explore for More—Why the Biggest Diamonds May Be in Your Own Backyard

Main Entry: ex·plore

Function: verb

1: to investigate, study, or analyze: look into—sometimes used with indirect questions

2: to become familiar with by testing or experimenting

Once you have gone through your first six PRECISE Actions and have some agreement with your customer about your next course of action, there is one more thing to do. *Explore* for more business. And I mean now. Yes, immediately after you have either gotten an order, a follow-up appointment, or a "Go to hell," your job is not done. As the definition of "explore" states, it's time to investigate, study, analyze, and look into with indirect (or direct) questions.

Look No Further

When you are finished presenting your solution to one prospect, it's time to look for another prospect, right? But why look? That "another" is standing right in front of you. Because most salespeople these days represent more than one product or solution, it is essential that they use their time in front of a prospect not only as selling time but also as prospecting time. Now I know you might be saying, "Sullivan, when I have a customer in front of me, I try to stay focused on the reason I am there. If I have a demonstration on one product or solution, I want to make sure that I sell that one first before I try to sell them something else."

Okay, I agree…to an extent. I am not asking you to risk your objective. I am, however telling you that too much business is left on the table because salespeople are too apprehensive to explore for more while that warm body is standing right in front of them. The benefits of exploring, in the form of more sales and higher commission checks, outweigh the risk of angering your customer. One of my goals in PRECISE Selling is to get salespeople to perform income-generating activities that they have not been comfortable doing.

Real versus Imaginary

There are two types of prospects, real prospects and imaginary prospects. Real ones are standing right in front of you or on the other end of the phone. Imaginary ones are a product of wishful thinking. While top performers love any prospect, they spend much more time with the ones that they can actually see and feel.

Imagine being a famous musician that fills a concert hall. You walk on stage with a list full of beautiful songs. But instead of playing all of them, you play just one, for fear of "overdoing it." You would rather just look for another audience to share that one song with, even if it takes a while. Well guess what, you just walked away from the audience that was right in front of you, and one that would probably love to hear more of what you have to offer. Hey, Maestro, give it a shot. Who knows? The manager of that concert hall just might book you for the rest of the year, saving you from ever having to look for another "gig" elsewhere again.

So when faced with the choice between prospecting for more business within the same account, or looking elsewhere, just remember:

> A prospect is only a real prospect when he is your audience.

Make Your Job Easier

Salespeople spend countless hours prospecting, cold calling, and doing everything possible to get in front of potential clients to deliver their message. When they finally get that appointment with a new prospect, there's a feeling of elation that they have accomplished something…and they have. I do not mean to knock new account prospecting. I do, however, mean to point you in a better direction. When given the choice between prospecting in existing accounts versus cold calling, which would you prefer? I know my answer. While PRECISE Selling is saying less while saying more, it is also taking the path of least resistance on the way to more sales. So if your objective this year is to increase your sales by 20 percent, explore for diamonds within your existing account base first, and then turn to new account prospecting.

Acre of Diamonds

There once was an African farmer who had heard tales of others making millions by discovering diamond mines. He became so excited at the thought of getting rich that he sold his farm and used the money to explore the African continent in search of the valuable gems.

Unfortunately for him, he never found any diamonds and he died a despondent and dejected man. Meanwhile, the man who had purchased the farm discovered a beautiful rock while crossing one of the streams on his newly acquired property.

The rock was so beautiful that he placed it on his fireplace mantel so that he could admire it. Several weeks later a visitor noticed the rock and nearly fainted from what he saw. The rock turned out to be one of the largest diamonds ever discovered. And it came from a small stream filled with many more large and precious stones. The man's small farm became one of the most productive diamond mines in all of Africa and he became a very rich man.

Dr. Russell Conwell, founder of Temple University, used this story in the mid-1800s to raise millions of dollars to help fund the formation of the school. "We need not waste our lives looking elsewhere for better opportunities," Dr. Conwell told his audiences.

I love this story because it has so many applications. Specifically, it reminds us, as salespeople, to keep our eyes and ears peeled for opportunities that exist right in front of us. It reminds us there may be "diamonds" within our existing accounts and that before we go exploring elsewhere, we must explore every inch of our own "farms."

Sara, a good friend of mine, is a sales rep for a medical distribution company that sells everything from cotton balls to heart monitors for physician clinics. A few years back, she had just been trained on a new device that was used to check a patient's blood pressure, blood oxygen level, and pulse. Sara was very excited to get out in the field and begin promoting it, and saw this as the perfect product to help open doors to new prospects. She came out of the sales gates hot by selling six devices to five different new accounts during the first two weeks. It was during week three that she learned of the lost diamond.

While she was busy trying to sell the device in newer accounts, Sara's biggest customer placed an order with her biggest competitor for twelve similar systems. Although she had a meeting with the same customer on another topic only days earlier, she neglected to Explore and engage the customer about the new product. When I asked Sara why she didn't mention it to her biggest account, she said that she thought for sure that they wouldn't be interested. She also mentioned that she sold them some high dollar equipment only weeks earlier and did not want to seem pushy. What's the message here?

> Look for the diamonds on your own farm
> before going to your neighbors.

What Instruments Do You Need to Explore?

You don't need a compass and a telescope, but you do need the essentials.

- Explorer's Attitude—This is your most important instrument. Your explorer's attitude should be "Christopher Columbus-like," and your purpose should be to seek out as much business as you can possibly find in any existing account. Even when others are telling you "The account is flat, Christopher. It's too dangerous to explore," don't believe them. Imagine where this thinking would have gotten Christopher—and many of us, for that matter!
- Risk-Taker's Attitude—Wayne Gretzky, perhaps the best hockey player ever to wear skates, reported the comment of an early coach who was frustrated with his lack of scoring in an important game. The coach made his point when he said, "You miss 100 percent of the shots you never take." So go ahead and ask for more business as often as you can. (I have faith in your ability to know when to back off.)

- Number Two Objective—Earlier we discussed the importance of setting an objective for your sales call. That objective is often focused on only one product or service. While having one objective is essential, having two objectives is exceptional. Objective number two should be to explore for added business beyond objective number one.
- Exploration Literature—Come prepared with extra selling materials like literature and brochures. And make them easy to get to when it is exploration time. Keep them in the same location in your briefcase or presentation binder so you don't find yourself clumsily fumbling for them.

Launch the USS Exploration

Once you have Secured and Advanced (PRECISE Action # 6), your sales call is pretty much over…so your prospect thinks! Hopefully, by this point, you would have done a good job at convincing them that your intent was to serve them, not sell them. If you have, then they should already be defenseless. (P.S. Your job was to sell them, they just don't need to know it.) But you can make them even more defenseless, which will, in return, buy you just a few extra minutes to explore for more business. Here are the steps to exploring.

- Thank your prospects for the time they gave you.
- Act like you are finished by putting some papers away or by beginning to pack up (don't do this too long; you might lose them) If you are phone selling, just ignore this step.
- Say these words, "I am curious . . ."
- Engage them with Questions and Curiosity.

Here is essentially what happened. You have already gone through PRECISE Actions numbers 1–6. You get to Action # 7 and it throws you right back up to Action #3.

1. Prepare
2. Respect and Trust
3. Engage with Questions and Curiosity
4. Convey Solution
5. Indecision—Overcome Yours and Theirs
6. Secure Agreement and Advance
7. Explore (by going back to Action #3)

So in essence, PRECISE Action #7 is just the beginning of the process again, except for having to do steps #1 and #2. I call this an E-Action.

For Every Exploration, There is an Equal E-Action

Let's say you sell life insurance and just sold a policy to a gentleman with a wife and three kids. You just finished your first six PRECISE Actions and your presentation was pure poetry. You asked for an agreement and sold the policy using one of your famously PRECISE Detail/Two-Choice Questions. You now are faced with two choices.

1. Thank the good Lord above and get the heck out of there.

2. Thank the good Lord above and explore for more business.

You go for choice number two because it will mean more money in your pocket. You have just closed a sale with the prospect so the stage is already set for you to try to get even more business. You are prepared with all the necessary materials and the prospect already likes you—it's time to explore! You thank him for the time he gave you, put some papers away, and move in.

You have determined that it would make a lot of sense for your prospect's wife to have insurance coverage as well. Should anything happen to her, it appears that it would greatly affect the financial condition of the family. An E-Action takes place and you are right back to PRECISE Action #3, "Engage with Questions and Curiosity."

You: "Joe, would you be interested in hearing how we could do an even more comprehensive job at protecting your family should tragedy strike?" (Good Engagement Question to gain curiosity.)

Joe: "Sure, but I thought I had enough coverage?"

You: "What are you *currently* doing to protect your family should anything happen to your wife?" (CLEAR Questioning at its finest)

JOE: Well, I guess not much."

YOU: "Have you *looked* at or considered a policy for your wife Susan?

JOE: "I guess I hadn't thought of it. She works part-time but does bring in a pretty good chunk of our income. If anything ever happened to her, I might have trouble paying the bills."

Okay, I think you get my point. The process has begun all over, and you can now provide added value to your prospect while increasing the size of your income. As the famous cliché goes, "That is a win/win!"

Two Ways to Explore

There are two ways to explore for extra business with an existing prospect. There is what I call Focused Exploration and Open Exploration. Both types of exploration need to be performed in a way that does not appear pushy. Remember, you have worked hard to bring the defensive walls of your prospect down, and if you are to be a successful explorer, you need to keep those walls down.

Focused Exploration

This occurs when you are looking for specific information that will lead your prospect toward the product or service of your choice. For instance, you just sell a new computer and are hoping to lead them toward buying a new color printer. Or you sell a new Stress Test EKG System and you ask questions designed at piquing their interest about buying a new defibrillator, should anyone go into cardiac arrest while on the treadmill. Focused Explorations include questions that will create curiosity about what you hope to sell, and get your customer thinking in a specific way.

The Engagement Question used in the life insurance sale above is an example of Focused Exploration because it purposely leads the prospect toward a specific discussion.

Open Exploration

This is less specific but is even more effective at getting your customer to express any Observable Needs that exist. For instance, Welch Allyn is a medical device company that manufactures hundreds of products. A Welch Allyn salesperson can walk into a family practice office for a specific device demonstration, and then explore to gain interest in over a dozen different products.

While a Focused Exploration Engagement Question would be one that leads the customer toward one specific product, an Open Exploration would instead attempt to get the customer to tell them where they plan to spend money next. It is also much more direct.

An example would be, "Mary, do you currently have money set aside in the budget for any other equipment?"

If an Observable Need exists, and you have a product that fulfills that need, yipee! You're in the game.

Another effective way to explore is to introduce your customer to your comprehensive catalog. This is effective when you sense that your prospect has little time left to spend with you. Take thirty seconds to flip the catalog around while you hold it. Do not hand it to them. While keeping control of the catalog, thumb through a few pages that you think might be of interest to your customer. You will be surprised at how many of your products or services pique their interest.

Exploring Problems

What if you have not sold solution number one yet? Use your best judgment when exploring. I like to err on the "go for it" side by exploring as often as possible with as many prospects as possible. But there are times when it makes sense to stay focused on carrying out objective number one before exploring for extra business.

What if your solution is not perfect for them? If you have been PRECISE, have not wasted their time, and have not tried to force-feed your solution, even the prospect that tells you, "It won't work," might still be willing to help you. Just because one of your products or services did not fulfill the customer's needs, this does not disqualify you from finding another need and fulfilling it. This is one of the advantages of always bringing with you Objective Number Two. If Objective Number One blows up in your face, the game is not over. You can still make something happen with some good old-fashioned exploration.

Explore for Referrals

Another great way to increase your business is to ask your prospects if they know of anyone else that would be interested in a solution they just learned about. If they like what you had to say, and jumped on board, why wouldn't they give you the names of others that might also find benefits in your solution?

If they liked you, but didn't think your product was the perfect solution, then they just might feel bad enough to hand over the names of some other folks that might make good prospects.

Many salespeople call on large companies with many different departments. If you are one of these reps, be sure to explore for diamonds in other departments of your existing accounts. Get as many names and know as many people as possible in as many departments as possible. And if someone with whom you have a relationship gives you some referrals within their own company, ask them if they would call ahead and perhaps give you a "plug." Your new prospect will open up much more quickly if you came by recommendation.

There Ain't No Diamonds On My Farm!

If there ain't no diamonds on your farm, it's time to find a new farm that has them. Or if you don't even own a farm yet, you need to go find one and start digging. While calling on existing customers is often easier than cold calling, there is little better in sales than making something out of nothing. So look at cold calling as the most difficult yet most rewarding part of your job. And as we discussed in earlier chapters, every "no" you get means money in your pocket. Seek them out! Those no's do prevent you from wasting lots of time, so don't be afraid of them. With enough hard work, the day may come when *you* say "no" to new clients because you are so damn busy taking care of your existing ones.

I will reserve PRECISE Cold-Calling Techniques for another book, but this much-maligned sales practice is essential to successful selling. The seven PRECISE Actions are perfect for cold calling. Because time is often limited when trying to get a prospect interested in your solution, you need to be PRECISE. Stick to the seven PRECISE Actions and specifically become an expert at CLEAR Questioning. Those five questions flat-out work! They will open up your prospect and as a result help focus your presentation. When time is limited, every word from your lips must count.

PRECISE Action
#7 Review

- Explore for Diamonds.
- Thank your prospects for the time they gave you.
- Give the appearance that you are finished by putting some papers away or by beginning to pack up (don't do this too long; you might lose them). If you are phone selling, just ignore this step.
- Say these words, "I am curious . . ."
- Engage them with questions and curiosity.

Chapter Nineteen
PRECISE Call Sheets:
Your Eight-Cent Tool to Becoming
PRECISE and Staying PRECISE

Do you know what the problem with sales books and sales training courses is? Hungry salespeople read these things, and ambitious companies invest thousands of dollars on programs that do not "stick." I know I went through dozens of books and several seminars, picking out the good and weeding out the "cheesy" before putting only some of what I learned to work.

The problem is not with the salespeople and companies doing their best to improve. The problem lies with the sales programs that do little to tell you exactly how to remember what you learned. Maybe it's because the sales gurus would rather have you buy another book, or perhaps have your company invite them back for another $10,000 motivational session.

In this chapter, I will give you a tool to help you remember everything I've taught you in this book. Frankly, once I am done training a company for two and a half days, I prefer that they never spend another nickel with me again. Why? Because once the material is delivered, all it takes is commitment, dedication, practice, and a willingness to get over the "strange" feeling that comes the first few times you use the seven PRECISE Actions. But these are things that I cannot provide. They are buried deep within a salesperson or sales organization and need to be cultivated. When I see this real commitment made, real results soon follow. The return is always so much more than is ever expected.

There is no greater satisfaction for me than to follow up with a company with whom I gave a seminar, and find out the salespeople have "bought into" PRECISE Selling. The reason I get so pumped is because it is those same salespeople that have committed to the three Ps of PRECISE, and the seven PRECISE Actions, that do become their company's top performer in 20 days or less. So if you want to be one of those salespeople, I am telling you how. I am not telling you that PRECISE Selling is the only way to be your company's best, but I am telling you that it will produce the results you are looking for. I have seen the material in this book come to life in many salespeople's lives. Give it a shot to make your job more fun and more profitable.

The Challenge—Dedicate Yourself to Being PRECISE

I would like to propose a challenge. I challenge you over the next 20 working days (take the weekends off, please) to commit to what you have read in these pages. I know there is a lot of information and a lot of steps to remember, and I don't expect you to review multiple pages each day. Instead, I do recommend that you go to the end of each chapter and look at the PRECISE Actions Review Page. These pages contain the essential information that you need to store in your brains for 20 days. If you forget everything else, and remember only what is on those pages, you can still be PRECISE. Remember:

> ## 20 days

Do this and you will be your company's top performer. Keep doing it, and you will become famous in your industry. You will make more money, become more confident, and have loads more fun. If you hit a wall, email me at bsullivan@preciseselling.com, and I will help you. I am totally convinced the material in this book will change your sales life, and quite frankly, I would love to be a part of your success. It is why I love my profession. When you begin to dominate, and I know you will, you will become a runaway train. The dominating momentum that you will build will be difficult to stop, and what an awesome thing that is!

"I reckon I must have walked UNDER
that ladder to the top!"

The Tool to Becoming and Remaining PRECISE

I call this tool a PRECISE Call Sheet, and it is the single most effective
tool to becoming and remaining PRECISE. It is a single sheet of paper
that contains the seven PRECISE Actions and is designed to be used
before, during, and after a sales call.

PRECISE Call Sheet

Date: _____   New/ Existing: _____

Company: _____   Department: _____

Address: _____   City/Zip: _____

Contact: _____   Phone Number: _____

Call Objective: _____

1. Preparation: _____

2. Respect and Trust: _____
    • "Thank you for your time." _____ ⬭
    • "I know you are in a hurry. I can save you time by asking some
       quick questions." _____ ⬭

3. Engage with Questions and Curiosity
    • Cold Prospect
    "Would you be interested in hearing how we can?" _____ ⬭
    • Warm Prospect
    "What got you interested?" _____ ⬭
    "Have you already decided on the need for a product like this?" ⬭
    • Currently using: _____ ⬭
    • Looking at other solutions: _____ ⬭
    • Effective: _____ ⬭
    • Alter: _____ ⬭
    • Responsible: _____ ⬭

4. Convey Solution:
    Bullets: _____ ⬭
    _____ ⬭
    _____ ⬭
    _____ ⬭
    _____ ⬭

5. Indecision:
    • Stop: _____
    • Hear: _____
    • Ask: _____
    • Respond: _____
    • Pack It: _____

6. Secure Agreement and Advance: _____

7. Explore: _____

The PRECISE Call Book

The PRECISE Call Book is a binder that contains several pages of the PRECISE Call Sheet. This will become your diary of performance for the next 20 days and beyond.

You have two choices here. You can either produce your own PRECISE Book or you can order one by going to www.preciseselling.com. Here you can customize your own, and PRECISE Selling will produce one for you. If you choose to produce your own, I recommend going to www.precise selling.com/wcb/PRECISECallSheet.pdf and downloading a copy of the sheet. You can then go to any office supply store and buy a three-ring binder. Create a section for every product or service grouping you have. For instance, if you sell five specific products, create five different sections and separate them with a divider. Label them by product so they are easy to get to. Print off several PRECISE Call Sheets and insert them into each section. I like to have about ten sheets for each section.

Using the PRECISE Call Book Before a Call

Before entering your next sales call or before picking up the phone, open the PRECISE Call Book. There are some spaces provided where you can write in the information of the account that you are calling on. Just below that you will notice a space for you to write in your call objective. Be as specific as you can in this area. You will judge the success of your call based on this objective.

Take thirty seconds to review the seven PRECISE Actions. This will "limber up" your mind a bit and better prepare you to be PRECISE during the upcoming call. This entire process should take about two minutes and I assure you, that two-minute investment will set up the flow of your entire call. This sheet will be the one you come back to after the call to rate your performance in each area. So it may be helpful to look at this as your pre/post PRECISE Call Sheet.

Using a PRECISE Call Sheet During the Call

In previous chapters, we discussed the importance of taking notes. PRECISE Call Sheets make great notepads, and I have seen them work for many salespeople. I don't recommend, however, that you open the entire PRECISE Call Book in front of your customer. They might think you are about to take minutes for the meeting. Remember, you want to keep your presentation as professional, yet as nonthreatening as can be. Having said that, many PRECISE reps find it helpful to take one of the sheets out of their binder and slide it into, or on top of, any notepad that they otherwise might use.

This works especially well during the first 20 days when you are honing your skills. Without it, it can be difficult to remember all seven PRECISE Actions. If you have the PRECISE Call Sheet in front of you as a guide, it will assure that you use all seven Actions in a PRECISE and organized manner. While using it as a notepad, it will remind you of exactly where you are in the sales process.

Also, spaces are provided on the sheet where you can put down all the information that your prospect is giving you. And don't worry about them "seeing it." So what if they did? That sheet you are holding is nothing more than an excellent tool to help you better serve you customer. If you stick to the Actions on that sheet, your call will go more quickly, more smoothly, and more PRECISE-ly than ever before. While your competition is dropping dumb bombs, wasting customer time, and jumping around their presentation like an out of control firecracker, your words will be so damn PRECISE you will amaze even yourself.

I am not too concerned with what notes you write down, just that you write something down. We are all different. Some sheets look like the Gettysburg Address when the rep is finished with a call, and others have just a few notes scribbled on a few lines. Personally, I use it to jot information such as bullets, objections, names of decision-makers, follow-up information needed, etc. Remember, when used during the call, it's just a notepad, so don't get too hung up about where you are supposed to jot everything. The biggest role of this sheet during the call is to be there for you to glance at should you find yourself getting "lost." And you know exactly what I'm talking about, don't you? It's the point where you just hit a wall, don't know what to say, so you just jump back to your brochure or product and begin spewing features and benefits. Don't do it! From now on, when every fiber of you is telling you to begin "your bombing run," take a breath, glance at your PRECISE Call Sheet, and get back on track.

Also, notice the ⬭ to the right of some of the actions on the sheet. These are placed in areas to alert you of specific dialogue that you should have with your prospect. If you said those things or something close to them, then you carried out your objective for that specific PRECISE Action. These can then be marked off.

For instance, let's say you came into the call prepared, did a great job of Building Respect and Trust, and then checked off the box. Then you find yourself in the middle of your Engagement Questions. Oh no! You forget what question comes next. Don't sweat it. Just give your sheet a quick glance, and it will tell you what to ask next. If you checked off the boxes as you completed them (don't worry, you can do this without it seeming like you are doing a survey), your eyes will go right to the next question.

I have seen so many reps use this flawlessly, and the confidence they display just knowing it's there makes a big difference. I liken this to quarterback that has the playbook taped on an armband for him to reference during the game. He doesn't spend a ton of time looking at it, but by effectively using it, he is able to move the offense more efficiently up the field. Now I realize this may be radically different from what you are used to doing. Sure it is! You didn't buy this book to tell you to keep doing what you are doing, did you?

All I can tell you is that you need to study this sheet every day for twenty minutes during the first 20 days. You should be able to close your eyes and recite these steps quickly. While the sheet is nice to have in front of you, you should not fall in love with it. The customer wants to talk to *you*, not a trained monkey reading off a sheet! Remember, when used during the call, it is to function as a life vest when needed, and a notepad. Beyond that, use it anyway you want to be keep you organized and PRECISE. While PRECISE Selling is about adding some process to your sales life, it is not about turning us all into clones.

I will say this: of the students that I teach, about a third use a PRECISE Call Sheet during the first 20 days. Guess which third of my students become truly PRECISE. You got it! So commit to try it right now. If you would like to make some changes to the sheet to better suit you, go right ahead. Do whatever you want with it; just get those seven Actions on paper and keep them in front of you during your first 20 days. I cannot stress this enough.

Using the PRECISE Call Book After a Call

Once you get off the phone or back out into your car, open your call book and review that call sheet. Start at the top and take just a few seconds reviewing each PRECISE Action. Make some notes about the actions that you were happy with and about the ones that you wish to improve on. This process should take about two or three minutes, no more. Once again, these two or three minutes will separate you from the average salespeople working in your company and in your industry. It seems so simple, and yet I have seen no tool in our profession that does a better job at creating and preserving top performers. Let's take a look at what a "filled out" call sheet would look like.

PRECISE Call Sheet (filled out)

Date: *Dec 5, 2003*   New/ Existing: _____

Company: _____   Department: _____

Address: _____   City/Zip: _____

Contact: _____   Phone Number: _____

Call Objective: *Get order for 10 new systems* _____

1. Preparation: *Bring more brochures next time* _____

2. Respect and Trust: _____

   • "Thank you for your time." _____ ◯

   • "I know you are in a hurry. I can save you time by asking some quick
    questions." *Forgot to thank the customer but did nice job of bringing the walls down* ◯

3. Engage with Questions and Curiosity

   • Cold Prospect

   "Would you be interested in hearing how we can?" _____ ◯

   • Warm Prospect

   "What got you interested?" *Forgot — it would have opened him up* ◯

   "Have you already decided on the need for a product like this?" ◯

• Currently using: _____ ◯

• Looking at other solutions: _____ ◯

• Effective: _____ ◯

• Alter: _____ ◯

• Responsible: *Forgot to ask about decision-makers* ◯

4. Convey Solution:

   Bullets: *Good job. I received 5 bullets. Be sure to get agreements on all* ◯
     bullets in the future before moving ahead. ◯
     _____ ◯
     _____ ◯
     _____ ◯

5. Indecision:

   • Stop: *Too impatient when they had concern — chill out!* _____

   • Hear: _____

   • Ask: _____

   • Respond: _____

   • Pack It: *Don't forget to get confirmation of agreement before packing*

6. Secure Agreement and Advance: *Good use of Detail/Two-Choice Questions*

7. Explore: *Ask for referrals next time*

Let's Recap It

Okay, this is a typical "filled out" PRECISE Call Sheet. In this case, the sheet was used as a post-sale evaluation tool. You will notice a PRECISE objective and short comments next to the specific areas the salesperson wanted to make note of. I am not a stickler on how you use this call sheet. I have seen it customized and used a dozen different ways, but don't feel as if you need to write a novel when filling it out. In fact, make your sheet as PRECISE as possible. Write down only those things that you want to stand out as areas needed for improvement, or areas noting good selling behavior.

Within your first 20 days of using this sheet, you will notice many more "Forgot to . . ." comments than "Great jobs." But as you continue to use your book and your sheets, and focus on improving only one or two specific PRECISE Actions each call, soon your sheet will have a lot more positive comments than negative.

I love traveling with PRECISE salespeople 20 days after committing to the program. When I ask to see their books, and I slowly turn the pages, I can see the specific improvement that was made on each call. When I get to the last PRECISE Call Sheet, I often see little writing on the sheet. It is not because the rep has given up on being PRECISE. It is because they have arrived! As they review each PRECISE Action, they are nailing every one. I guess these PRECISE reps just get tired of writing down "Great job!"—and oh, what a problem to have.

What About Retail Sales?

If you are in retail sales, I realize that it will be a little difficult to be walking around the store with a PRECISE Call Book. So don't do it. I do recommend, however, that you evaluate your performance at the end of your sales day. Sum up your day worth of calls according to the seven Actions, and make a few notes in your book. And before your next sales day, look inside and see which specific areas you need to improve on. Take one or two of them, and concentrate on those actions during the day. At the end of the day, make some notes about your improvement in those specific areas. Did you perform more PRECISE-ly? What actions will you tackle next? By doing this, you will be more focused and conscientious about your sales behavior. Chances are you never looked at your sales day this specifically.

Manage Yourself

Have you ever had a sales manager travel with you in your car or sit next to you on the phone? If you have, you know that once the call is over, there will be a discussion about how it went. These conversations are rarely specific and often entail the sales manager preaching to the salesperson about what she should have done. The problem is that the instruction from the sales leader is rarely specific enough to help you make a wholesale improvement in your performance. Well, with the seven PRECISE Actions, who needs a sales manager? (Don't tell them I said this!)

What I mean is that you now have the tools to manage yourself. By evaluating your performance using the PRECISE Call Sheet after every call, *you* can have that sales discussion with…well…*you*. And you don't even have to wait for that wonderful day when you're manager stops by for a visit.

I will guarantee that if you commit to the seven PRECISE Actions today, and then you're manager travels with you 20 days from now, you are about to freak him out. When they see how PRECISE you are and how happy your customers are with the way you serve them, my friend, good things are about to happen. Watch! And as you uphold that commitment and hone your skills, by day 20 you will see the results. *You will be your company's top performer!*

The PRECISE Nerds

Okay, I admit it. I am a total techno geek. The only paper I usually like to touch is the sports section while throwing back my first mug of coffee in the morning. Beyond that, when it comes to record-keeping, account managing, sales projections, whatever, if it's not made up of bits and bytes, it scares the hell out of me. Maybe it's because I can no longer read my own handwriting. Anyway, if you are a similar nerd, and almost collapsed at the thought of carrying around a Call Sheet Book, fear not. While I don't think it makes sense to use your PDA or laptop computer to take notes while a prospect is telling you their wants and needs (there are geeks, and there are *serious geeks*, don't be the serious type), it might make sense for you to record post-call performance electronically. This way you can get back into your car after a sales call, pull up your call sheet, and quickly record what you did well and what areas you need to improve on.

If you prefer this method, email me at bsullivan@preciseselling.com and I will send you an Excel Spreadsheet or Word Document with the PRECISE Call Notes on it. This call sheet can also be easily transferred to your PDA with a software program called Documents to Go. Whatever method you choose to become PRECISE, be it old-school or nerd-school, do something.

Recap the Value of the Sheet

I will say it again. It is almost impossible to become PRECISE without using the PRECISE Call Sheet. So let's drill this into that "Aspiring to be PRECISE" head of yours:

- Use the Call Sheet to set an objective and to help you think about your PRECISE Actions before the call.
- Take notes.
- Evaluate your performance with the PRECISE Call Sheet.

---

20 days

Commit to what you have learned for 20 days, hone the skills, and then evaluate your sales performance after 20 days. Like many coaches in sports often say, "Take it one game at a time." Don't look toward the championship too early, or you will never get there. Look at each sales call as one game. Keep winning individual games and the rest will take care of itself. You will be your company's top performer. And practice. If somebody asked you after Day 20 to recite the seven PRECISE Actions, you should be able to recite them in about seven seconds. I am serious about this.

The objective is to get your mind thinking as quickly as possible during the call, and this starts with being able to recite the seven Actions quickly. Once you are able to do this, your mind will know exactly where to go, even without a PRECISE Call Sheet in front of you. When a customer throws you a fast one, you will remain disciplined and have confidence. Those seven PRECISE Actions will be the foundation that will keep you patient and in control of the call. With that control, you can lead your prospect to a sale. Without it, you cannot be PRECISE. I wish you tons of luck on your way to the top. With patience, determination, and practice, you are about to make a bigger name for yourself.

Practice

"I am a dancer. I believe that we learn by practice. Whether it means to learn to dance by practicing dancing or to live by practicing living, the principles are the same. In each, it is the performance of the dedicated, precise set of acts, physical or intellectual, from which comes shape of achievement, a sense of one being, a satisfaction of spirit. One becomes, in some area, an athlete of God."
—Martha Graham (1893–1991), American dancer and choreographer

PRECISE-ly said!

Epilogue
Sales Leaders and Managers: How to Help You and Your People Become Precision-Guided Sales Weapons

> "Coaching is giving your players a good design
> and getting 'em to play hard."
> —Bill Parcells, professional football coach

In the previous pages, I have given you the design known as PRECISE Selling. And of course, your job is to get your people to "play hard" every day, isn't it? Put PRECISE Selling and hard work together and you have a proven formula for success. If you can motivate your salespeople to totally commit to reviewing the material in *20 Days to the Top* on a daily basis for 20 days, you will have a company loaded with top performers.

For added support, send an email to marketing@preciseselling.com and include the names of your salespeople that have read the book. I will send them a new message each day, reminding them of the benefits of committing to the PRECISE Selling Formula. For your people that commit to the 20 days, unbelievable results are about to occur. Your C players will become B's or better. Your B players will become A's. And you will find that many of your A's will use PRECISE Selling to perform at the highest level more consistently.

And what about your performance as a sales leader? How can PRECISE Selling help you? Well the answer is simple, my friend. *You* have to be the best salesperson in your company. I don't mean you necessarily need to be the best at selling your company's product or service to the customer. I mean you need to be the best at selling an even more important product...your vision.

You see, it all starts with you. The people who work for you are the engine of your company. If they are not sold on you, your vision, your mission, your objectives, your purpose, and how it is in their best interest to "buy" what you are selling, then consistent success will be difficult to achieve. If you become effective at using the PRECISE Selling Formula with your own people, they will become happier "customers."

- Prepare: You will be better prepared when meeting with them.
- Respect and Trust: You will build greater respect and trust.
- Engage: You will better engage them with questions that will open them up and let them tell you where they need help. (You will be amazed how often it is exactly what you were thinking.)
- Convey: You will convey your solution in a way that has maximum impact to each individual employee.
- Indecision: You will overcome leadership-destroying indecision that leads to employee indecision.
- Secure: You will secure agreement and advance employee commitment.
- Explore: You will explore for ways to help your people and be more proactive about giving feedback.

I call this PRECISE Leadership but frankly, it is more about "selling" the benefits of following your lead.

> To be a great leader, you need to be a great salesperson.

So as you think about the material taught in this book, think about how it can help you better "sell" your message to your people. And as you improve, your salespeople will follow your lead.

Tools to Help You Become PRECISE
This Book
20 Days to the Top: How the PRECISE Selling Formula Will Make You Your Company's Top Sales Performer in 20 Days or Less will do two things for a salesperson/sales leader.

1. Introduce and explain the PRECISE Selling Formula.
2. Act as a reference guide for improvement that is easy to refer to.

PRECISE One-Hour Motivational Clinics

PRECISE Selling offers educational and entertaining sessions on a variety of topics. Brian Sullivan will learn the details of your business, industry, and competition, and customize a motivational and instructional clinic that will improve your people's skills immediately.

Half-Day Interactive Seminar

"Brian's four-hour presentation, during which he held our sales and customer service staff's attention throughout, was in a word——terrific!! Brian's presentation of the PRECISE Selling Formula to assist our sales staff in assessing customer needs and closing the sale leaves a lasting impression (which a year later we are still using). His ability to mix humor with the serious is extremely effective. His kinetic approach is enjoyable. His interaction with his audience without embarrassing participants produces very valuable feedback. I can honestly say he is as good as anyone that I have seen in my twenty-five years in the health care sales business."

—Miles Unobsky Theeman, COO, Affiliated Healthcare

Brian will delve more deeply into your business and the specific challenges you face daily. He will then customize a seminar within the framework of the PRECISE Selling Formula in a way that sends your people away with the specific tools to become top performers. Unlike many sales seminars, PRECISE Selling is easy to use, easy to remember, and easy to measure. This is important! Sales training is an investment, and nobody likes to waste money on tactics and strategies that are never used. With your help (and mine), you will give your people the tools to put more money in their pockets.

PRECISE Selling Camp

"Just *awesome!!* Your Selling Camp, using the PRECISE Selling technique for nineteen IMCO sales representatives, surpassed much more than we ever imagined. Without a doubt, you have touched their sales lives. The material and the techniques are right on target, but your masterful delivery and style of impacting a point made it alive to them."

—Yates Farris, Vice President, IMCO, Inc.

Sleeping bags are not required—just a total dedication to become the dominate player in your market or industry. This two and a half day seminar focuses more intensely on the seven PRECISE Actions and allows ample time for skill practice. Your people will walk away with much more than a dose of sales Viagra. They will have the formula and motivation to be top performers for months and years to come.

PRECISE Trainers Clinic

Learn to teach the PRECISE Selling Formula of Top Performers to your people. During this session, you will not only become PRECISE yourself, you will learn what it takes to teach your own people how to become top performers.

PRECISE Leadership Seminar

Learn the PRECISE Leadership Formula and discover new ways to "sell" your vision to the people you serve—your reps. This seminar focuses on more effective coaching techniques and will make you your company's top sales leader.

PRECISE DVDs and Videotapes

Do you often have new hires that need sales training? Do you need a refresher for your more seasoned reps? Invest in *20 Days to the Top* video DVDs and videotapes and be prepared to deliver tactical sales training on demand.

Audio CDs

Do your people spend lots of "windshield" time? *20 Days to the Top* is available on audio CD and turns those nonselling hours into productive, educational time. Your sales professionals will show up for their next sales call better prepared to serve their customers.

PRECISE Home Study Course

This is the "total package" for those looking to become PRECISE. It contains an eight hour home/road study course that includes:
• 8 Interactive video CDs
• 8 Hours of instruction downloaded from the Web
• 8 Audio CDs for the car
• 8 Hours of downloadable instruction (Great for your MP3 player)
• Instruction manual
• Online testing to check your progress
• Deck of Mem-Cards® "Cheat sheets in a deck of cards."

This is the most comprehensive sales training program available.

Contact Information

If you like what you have read and are interested in hearing how PRECISE Selling can help turn you and your people into top performers, please visit our website at www.preciseselling.com or contact:

PRECISE Selling
286 W. Highland Ridge Court
Village of Loch Lloyd, MO 64012
Office: (913) 530-8894
Fax: (816) 318-8206
Email: marketing@preciseselling.com

Thanks for giving us a look and best of luck on your climb to the top.

A

B

C

F

fact-finding questions, 35
Faker, 43
fear, 57, 157, 190, 192
fishing, 21–29
flea, 10
fly, 9
football, 92–93, 100, 101, 129–130

G

Gardner, John W, 89, 171
gastroenterologist, 14
Giuliani, Rudy, 56, 57

H

habit, 10, 18, 40, 43, 68, 74, 77, 84, 89, 90, 91, 96, 138, 161, 187
handshake, 112–113

I

Internet, 70, 83, 84
interrupter, 44

J

jackass, 80, 102, 103, 115
Jefferson, Thomas, 79

L

laughter, 15
leaders, 8, 33, 85, 86, 99, 148, 215
literature, 22, 83, 106
Lombardi, Vince, 8, 59, 97, 100, 101
London, Jack, 67
Luther, Martin, 11

M

magnet, 31, 71–72
Marshall, George, 41
Melaro, Tony, 73
memory, 41, 46–49, 51, 90, 125
memory test, 47–49
Midmark, 72–73
Mizner, Wildon, 44
monkeys, 61–62
mopes, 21
Moran, John, 71, 99
MTV, 55, 80

N

Neg-ceptionist, 26
newsletter, 70

O

objective, 7, 9, 13, 40, 62, 72, 73, 92, 93, 99–101, 107, 115, 122, 124,
    130, 134, 136, 138, 145, 151, 152, 157, 160, 164, 168, 185, 186,
    188, 190, 192, 193, 195, 198, 205, 207, 210, 212
office mangler, 27
opinion, 22, 23, 25, 26, 28, 29, 44, 56, 84, 117, 154, 175

P

peace of mind, 56, 57, 122
pessimism, 58
PIC Knowledge, 53, 54, 64, 77, 79–86, 133, 163, 168
plateau, 17
Popeye, 15, 16, 18
posture, 53, 56–77, 87, 158
PRECISE Actions, 3, 38, 40, 53, 54, 87–96, 97, 123, 141, 142, 146, 166, 174, 188, 191, 195, 196, 199, 201–212, 218
PRECISE Call Sheets, 3, 201–213
preparation, 97–107, 204, 209
probing question, 129
proctologist, 13
pussycat, 105

R

Raleigh, Sir Walter, 11
rat, 104
resistance, 32, 119, 143, 188, 193
respect, 7, 35, 56, 64, 66, 87, 99, 104, 105, 109–119, 123, 130, 135, 137, 139, 143, 158, 164, 175, 195, 216
rookie, 3–4
Roosevelt, Franklin, 11

S

scapegoat, 106
scheduled appointment, 115–117
secure agreement, 7, 179
sheep, 105–106
shut up, 16
silence, 45–46
slot machine, 111
smile, 4, 14, 21, 25, 43, 46, 59, 60, 67, 104, 109, 112, 159, 162, 182, 183

About the Author

Brian Sullivan is a member of the National Speakers Association and one of the medical industry's most prominent and sought-after sales and leadership trainers. *20 Days to the Top* details Brian's journey, and highlights the sales methods that transformed him from top sales performer to an international authority on effective selling behavior. His success as an expert on selling now extends well beyond the medical market and his methodology is now delivered to dozens of industries. Over a fifteen-year sales career, Brian gained his expertise by selling equipment and consulting with physician offices and hospitals as a sales representative, equipment specialist, sales manager, and director of sales training for Welch Allyn, Inc., a leading medical device manufacturer.

As a sales representative, Brian was awarded Welch Allyn's President's Cup in 1996, recognizing the company's top performance in attitude, aptitude, and performance, and was consistently Welch Allyn's top high-end capital equipment performer. Though his stellar selling reputation resulted in continual promotions, each new opportunity was developed with an eye to maximizing and disseminating Brian's gift in the sales training arena. In 1996, Brian codeveloped and implemented the sales training program that is delivered to Welch Allyn's sales and marketing staff, both domestically and internationally. Today, Brian delivers over 100 presentations a year to companies that have an intense desire to turn their people into precision-guided sales weapons. And by bringing his presentations to life with comical anecdotes, humor, and passion, PRECISE Selling is a message that fundamentally changes the way salespeople and sales leaders view their careers.

When not speaking to companies and associations, Brian also spreads his business message over the air waves by hosting a radio talk show called *Entrepreneurial Moments*. This AM radio show explores various topics related to the entrepreneurial experience in conversations with successful business owners and risk takers.

Brian lives in Kansas City, Missouri, with his wife and two children.